analyzes support for communism and fascism in several countries in relation to rates of urbanization and industrialization, unemployment, suicide and homicide, and other phenomena.

The theory of mass society reveals many new clues to the origins and nature of mass political movements. *The Politics of Mass Society* contains the most complete analytical study of the theory of mass society in print.

PROFESSOR WILLIAM KORNHAUSER teaches in the Department of Sociology at the University of California, Berkeley. He also taught at Columbia University and the Salzburg Seminar in American Studies in Austria. During 1954-55 he was a Fellow at the Center for Advanced Study in the Behavioral Sciences. He is an associate editor of the *Pacific Sociological Review.*

THE POLITICS
OF MASS SOCIETY

By William Kornhauser

THE FREE PRESS OF GLENCOE

TO MY FATHER

Among the laws that rule human societies there is one which seems to be more precise and clear than all others. If men are to remain civilized or to become so, the art of associating together must grow and improve in the same ratio in which the equality of conditions is increased.

De Tocqueville

Preface

THIS BOOK examines historical and contemporary situations marked by widespread readiness to abandon constitutional modes of political activity in favor of uncontrolled mass action. It analyzes the sources of support for communism, fascism, and other popular movements that operate outside of and against the institutional order. At the same time, this study attempts to specify social conditions that sustain liberal democratic institutions. The sources of strength and weakness in democratic political systems are sought in the social structure. The central argument of this study is that insofar as a society is a *mass society*, it will be vulnerable to political movements destructive of liberal democratic institutions; while insofar as a society is *pluralist*, these institutions will be strong. A major implication of this argument is that the theory of mass society and the theory of social pluralism employ similar categories of analysis, and therefore are but two statements of a more general theory. The formulation and application of this general theory constitute the principal aim of the present work. Voting statistics and other kinds of empirical material are used to help specify the theory; rigorous testing of the theory remains to be done. Therefore, this study is offered as a tentative statement of a theory which, it is hoped, will lead to further research and theoretical analysis.

This study grew out of my association with a committee for an inventory of knowledge on political behavior, Seymour

Lipset, chairman, which was supported by a grant from the Behavioral Sciences Division of the Ford Foundation to the Bureau of Applied Social Research, Columbia University. I gratefully acknowledge the support I received from this committee. I also am grateful to the Center for Advanced Study in the Behavioral Sciences for a year in a stimulating environment which greatly facilitated my research, and to the University of California for a grant from the Institute of Social Science and for a Faculty Fellowship to complete the study. I am greatly indebted to James Coleman, Alex Garber, Arthur Kornhauser, Ruth Kornhauser, Paul Lazarsfeld, Seymour Lipset, Leo Lowenthal, and Philip Selznick for their valuable suggestions and criticisms.

WILLIAM KORNHAUSER

Berkeley, California

Acknowledgments

THE AUTHOR and The Free Press acknowledge, with thanks, the permissions granted by publishers and copyright holders to quote from sources referred to in this volume. Specifically, thanks are due the following:

Alfred A. Knopf, Inc., for permission to quote from *Democracy in America*, by Alexis de Toqueville;

The American Jewish Committee, for permission to quote from "Poujade," by Herbert Luethy, in *Commentary*, Vol. XXI (April, 1956);

Confluence, for permission to quote from "Totalitarianism and Freedom," by Raymond Aron, Vol. II (June, 1953);

Cornell University Press, for permission to quote from *Communism in Western Europe*, by Mario Einaudi, J. Domenach, and A. Garoschi;

Europa Verlag A. G. Zurich, for permission to quote from *The Revolution of Nihilism*, by Hermann Rauschning;

Harcourt Brace and Company, for permission to quote from *The New Men of Power*, by C. Wright Mills;

Harper and Brothers, for permission to quote from *Capitalism, Socialism, and Democracy*, by Joseph Schumpeter;

Harvard University Press, for permission to quote from *The French Labor Movement*, by Val Lorwin;

Longmans, Green and Company, Inc., for permission to quote from *Politics in Post-War France*, by Philip Williams;

Oxford University Press, Inc., for permission to quote from *The Power Elite*, by C. Wright Mills;

Public Opinion Quarterly, for permission to quote from "A Review of Swen Rydenfell's *Communism in Sweden*," by W. Phillips Davison, Vol. XVIII (1954–55);

The RAND Corporation, for permission to quote from *West German Leadership and Foreign Policy*, edited by Hans Speier and W. Phillips Davison;

Random House, Inc., for permission to quote from *The Social Background of Political Decision-Makers*, by Donald R. Matthews;

Routledge and Kegan Paul, Ltd., for permission to quote from *Man and Society in an Age of Reconstruction*, by Karl Mannheim;

The University of Chicago Press, for permission to quote from "Small Businessmen, Political Tolerance, and Support for McCarthy," by Martin Trow, in the *American Journal of Sociology*, Vol. LXIV (1958; copyright 1958 by the University of Chicago) ;

George Wahr Publishing Company, for permission to quote from *British Election Studies, 1950*, by James Pollock, *et al.;*

Yale University Press for permission to quote from *Citizens Without Work*, by E. Wight Bakke.

Contents

List of Tables

Introduction

IT HAS BECOME a commonplace to speak of modern society as "mass society" in order to stress its size and complexity. From this point of view, the United States and the Soviet Union are prototypes of the mass society. Such a use of the term does not add to our understanding of modern society. By covering whatever is observed in large and complex systems, "mass society" becomes merely a short-hand expression for the modern world. If the United States is observed to be pluralist, for example, then the inference is made that "mass society" may be pluralist. Or, if the Soviet Union is judged to be totalitarian, then "mass society" may be totalitarian. Used in this manner, the concept has little analytical value.

This is to be regretted because the idea of mass society has a very rich history as a conception of *specific* tendencies which undermine freedom in the modern world. This intellectual heritage is denied by those who would assimilate everything "modern" to the concept, and so are the problems around which the idea has been developed. A central aim of this study is to distinguish between mass tendencies and pluralist tendencies in modern society, and to show how social pluralism, but not mass conditions, supports liberal democracy. This effort is based on the premise that the strength of democratic institutions depends on the underlying social structure, and *not* on the idea that modern democracy is everywhere in peril. Thus, it is not to be assumed that the United States, for example, is the prototype of mass society, or that democratic institutions in the United States are not strong. Those who reject the theory when they observe anti-mass tendencies in America, England, or elsewhere confound the general criteria of mass society with the particular case. The theory does assert that contemporary societies are especially likely to develop properties of mass society, unless strong counter-tendencies exist; but it does not imply that all modern societies manifest these properties in the same degree. The idea of mass society is a diagnosis of certain underlying tendencies in the modern world, as well as a set of criteria for measuring the extent of these tendencies in specific cases.

"Mass society," then, is not to be identified as modern society. Neither is it to be confounded with a particular class. The "masses" are not to be confused with the working class, nor are "mass movements" to be identified with social movements based on the working class. This study develops the proposition that under certain conditions any or all classes may give rise to masses, in the sense of large numbers of people who are not integrated into any broad social groupings, including classes.[1] It shall be further argued that totalitarian movements are fundamentally mass movements rather than class movements.[2] Specifically, although fascism tends to recruit a disproportionate number of its adherents from the middle class and communism attracts more of its adherents from the working class, these movements cannot be understood merely as political expressions of the working class and the middle class, respectively. For in both cases, a large proportion of the movement is composed of people who possess the weakest rather than the

---

1. This is not to deny that certain classes are more likely to give rise to masses than others. On the contrary, this study explores in great detail the differential vulnerability of classes to mass phenomena. See especially Part III, below.

2. For a critical evaluation of the utility of class analysis for the study of totalitarian movements, see Bendix (1952).

strongest class ties. Furthermore, both movements tend to draw many adherents from all major social classes. This common property of a mass (rather than class) base helps to explain the *similarity* between fascism and communism, namely, their *totalitarianism*.[3]

Classes subsist along with masses but they become less effective determinants of political behavior insofar as society is a mass society. The decisive difference is between the behavior of people who form a mass and that of people who are attached to independent groups. Therefore, a second aim of this study is to show how variations in the character of the individual's social relations influence his receptivity or resistance to the appeals of totalitarianism.

The primary utility of mass analysis centers in its power to explain *crisis politics* and the extremist response, whereas class analysis would appear to be more useful in the area of *routine politics*. For if class theory began as an explanation of economic crisis and political change, it increasingly finds effective use as a mode of analysis of political alignments under more or less stable conditions of industrial society. This is demonstrated in the burgeoning literature on the bases of electoral cleavage within modern Western

---

3. Carl Friedrich (1954, p. 48) recently has distinguished between works on fascism and communism which stress their similarities and works which stress the distinctiveness of fascism: "Sigmund Neumann, in *Permanent Revolution* (1942), treats them [fascism and communism] as basically alike. . . . Franz Neumann, in *Behemoth* (1942 and later), on the other hand, deals with the Hitler dictatorship as something quite distinctive, essentially the creation if not the creature of big business, the bureaucracy, and the army. Among earlier works, Alfred Cobban's *Dictatorship, Its History and Theory* (1939) . . . [treats] Fascist and Communist dictatorship as alike. . . . Two other volumes also stressed the connection between Fascist and Communist dictatorship: *Dictatorship in the Modern World* (edited by Guy Stanton Ford, 1935 and 1939), and Hans Kohn's *Revolutions and Dictatorships* (1939). Among the books emphasizing either explicitly or by implication the distinctness of fascism, mention might be made of E. B. Ashton (pseudonym), *The Fascist—His State and His Mind* (1937); Herbert W. Schneider, *Making the Fascist State* (1928); G. A. Borgese, *Goliath, the March of Fascism* (1937); Max Ascoli and Arthur Feiler, *Fascism for Whom?* (1938); and several books on Nazi Germany, including Frederick L. Schumann, *The Nazi Dictatorship* (1935 and later); Fritz Morstein Marx, *Government in the Third Reich* (1936 and later); Karl Loewenstein, *Hitler's Germany* (1939 and later)."

democracies. The present study seeks to show that mass theory is useful for the analysis of sources of extremist tendencies in these same societies.

Mass society is not synonymous with industrial society nor with the working class in industrial society. It also is to be differentiated from totalitarian society. Many theorists of mass society are prone to liken totalitarian societies to mass societies. This conception leads to certain major difficulties of analysis, since the kinds of social process they identify as mass phenomena pertain primarily to weaknesses in democratic institutions which make them vulnerable to capture by totalitarian elites, rather than to the nature of totalitarian institutions themselves. Confusion results when the same concept is used to explain both the weakness of democratic institutions and the functioning of totalitarian institutions. Therefore, a third aim of this study is to distinguish between mass institutions and totalitarian institutions, and to specify the relations between them. Mass society will be conceived of as a set of conditions under which democratic institutions are vulnerable to totalitarianism, rather than as a set of conditions underlying totalitarian institutions.

The theory of mass society does not imply a low valuation of democracy, but merely claims that certain tendencies in modern society must be checked if democracy is to remain strong. These tendencies are the loss of autonomy on the part of elites and the loss of independent group life on the part of non-elites. The atomized society invites the totalitarian movement, which provides both pseudo-authority in the form of the charismatic leader and pseudo-community in the form of the totalitarian party. Since democracy may encourage the atomization of society, it may carry with it certain self-defeating tendencies. Democracy of course also contains many self-sustaining processes. For example, it also encourages the formation of multiple elites and associations which help to maintain a wide dispersal of power. The theory of mass society does not imply that any given democracy may not successfully sustain itself, but only that those factors with which it is concerned cannot be ignored in any assessment of the main paths along which democratic societies may move.

This study attempts to account for some of the major social factors that weaken democratic order by applying the theory of mass society to a variety of empirical materials. It is an effort to gauge the plausibility of this theory as an explanation for a limited range of phenomena. It proceeds first by formulating the theory of mass society in light of its intellectual roots; and second by applying the theory to political movements in Western society. Part I delineates the major properties of mass society which make it vulnerable to anti-democratic movements. Part II examines conditions under which these movements (especially communism and fascism) have gained strength at the expense of democratic institutions. Part III analyzes the social composition of these movements, that is, the kinds of people who flock to mass movements bent on destroying democratic society. The Conclusion summarizes the implications of the theory of mass society for the conditions that support liberal democratic order, and raises certain questions about the present situation in American society.

PART I

THEORY

OF MASS SOCIETY

Chapter 1

Two Views
of Mass Society

THE THEORY of mass society has two major intellectual sources, one in the nineteenth century reaction to the revolutionary changes in European (especially French) society, and the other in the twentieth century reaction to the rise of totalitarianism, especially in Russia and Germany. The first and major source may be termed the *aristocratic* criticism of mass society; the second, the *democratic* criticism of mass society. The first centers in the intellectual defense of elite values against the rise of mass participation. The second centers in the intellectual defense of democratic values against the rise of elites bent on total domination. The defensive posture of the aristocrats has been adopted by democrats who, having won the nineteenth century war of ideas and institutions with the former, now seek to preserve their values against the totalitarian challenge.

Not all intellectual rejections of revolutionary change have been based on the idea of mass society. Criticisms of nineteenth century trends that may properly be termed theories of mass society found the decisive social process to be *the loss of exclusiveness of elites and the rise of mass participation in cultural and political life.* Burckhardt (1955) *

---

* Names and dates in parentheses refer to the items in the list of references appearing at the end of the book.

and Gustave Le Bon (1947) were among the leading aristocratic critics of mass tendencies in the nineteenth century;
Ortega y Gasset (1932), and Karl Mannheim (1940, pp.
79-96), in his discussions of elites, are twentieth century
representatives of this approach.[1]

Similarly, not all democratic criticisms of totalitarianism
are based on a theory of mass society. Those which may
properly be termed theories of mass society find the decisive
social process to be *the loss of insulation of non-elites and
the rise of elites bent on total mobilization of a population.*
Emil Lederer (1940) and Hannah Arendt (1951) are leading representatives of this conception of the nature of mass
society.[2]

Paradoxical as it may appear to be, these democratic
critics have come to rely heavily on the intellectual weapons
employed by aristocratic thinkers against the rising flood
of democratic ideologists during the nineteenth century.
The central idea taken over by these democratic theorists
from their aristocratic critics is that *the preservation of
critical values (especially freedom) requires the social insulation of those segments of society that embody them.*
Aristocratic and democratic critics of mass society agree on
this, even as they disagree on the content of the values to be
preserved—especially the nature of freedom—and, correspondingly, on the segments of society that embody them.

The aristocratic notion of freedom emphasizes the conditions that permit men to act as they *ought* to act, that is, in
accordance with standards of right conduct. Mannheim has
noted that this idea of freedom is counterposed to an egalitarian conception: "Men, . . . [the aristocratic theorists] claimed

1. Catholic critics of nineteenth century society, like Bonald and De Maistre
share certain views with aristocratic critics. So do such aesthetic critics as
Arnold. In the most general sense, all anti-bourgeois intellectuals of the
nineteenth century shared certain ideas which were congenial to a theory of
mass society. For a brief review of conservative ideas since the French
Revolution, see Viereck (1956).

2. Arendt's recent discussion (1956) of authority closely follows the
aristocratic criticism of mass society.

are essentially *unequal,* unequal in their gifts and abilities, and unequal to the very core of their beings" (1953, p. 106). Standards of right conduct are most highly developed in the upper reaches of society, and therefore the "true bearers," the "true subjects" of liberty are the "organic communities" of aristocratic elites. "The 'liberty' of the different estates under feudalism which meant their 'privileges,' and the distinctly qualitative and non-egalitarian flavour which was contained in the medieval concept, is here revived once more" (Mannheim, 1953, p. 107). The traditional order based on moral law insulates aristocratic elites and thereby preserves liberty.

The democratic notion of freedom, on the other hand, implies the minimizing of social control (including that of the traditional order), that is, the removal of as many external constraints on the individual as is consistent with the freedom of his fellows. Freedom so conceived is dependent on *equality of rights.* This value is embodied in the whole community. Therefore, it is the independent group life of the non-elite which functions to preserve liberty, as independent groups insulate people from domination by elites.

In sum, these two versions of the mass society differ in their conception of freedom and the social foundations of freedom. One sees mass society as a set of conditions under which elites are exposed to mass pressures. The other conceives of mass society as a set of conditions under which non-elites are exposed to elite pressures. Nevertheless, they share a common image of mass society as the *naked society,* where the direct exposure of social units to outside forces makes freedom precarious. We shall attempt to formulate a general theory of mass society that incorporates elements from both the aristocratic and democratic criticism. This is our objective in Part I of the present study.

But to reach this goal, it is necessary to explicate partial and polemical versions of the theory. Therefore, we consider first the major argument of the aristocratic criticism of mass society, and then we analyze the democratic criticism of mass society. First a word about the bases for distinguishing these two views.

Our interest is in analyzing the theoretical basis of each approach, rather than in examining the value orientation typically associated with each of them. The two approaches have been distinguished according to whether the condition of elites or the condition of non-elites is identified as the basic criterion of "mass society." This means that any theory that locates the decisive feature of mass society in the exposure of accessible elites to mass intervention is classified as "aristocratic," while any theory that locates the essential feature of mass society in the exposure of atomized non-elites to elite domination is classified as "democratic." The choice of the terms "aristocratic" and "democratic" to describe these two theories should not obscure the fact that the classification is based on an *analytical* rather than a value distinction. However, there is an affinity between each of these theoretical positions and each value orientation. Most writers on mass society whose *theories* have focused on the loss of insulation of elites have also advocated aristocratic *values,* while most of those whose theories have focused on the loss of insulation of non-elites have also advocated democratic values. Nevertheless, there are some exceptions, for some writers hold values of the one type and expound theories of the other. When this occurs, the contributions are classified according to the theoretical, not the value, position of the writer. This explains why Mannheim, for example, is cited as a representative of the "aristocratic" approach; though committed to the preservation of democratic *values,* his *theory* of mass society tends to stress the way in which mass participation undermines elite functions.[3]

There is a second point, relating to the theoretical nature of the classification (rather than its value relevance), that

---

3. Critics of the theory of mass society generally fail to differentiate between the aristocratic and democratic versions of that theory. A recent example is Daniel Bell's critique (1956).

should be borne in mind. Our interest is in the logic of each argument, rather than in the work of particular theorists. A separate series of logically connected propositions about the nature of mass society is related to the major premise of each approach. A particular theorist may well incorporate aspects of both arguments in his writings, without thereby providing a clear outline of either argument or a general and systematic statement of the theory of mass society. It may sometimes happen, therefore, that the same writer is at one time cited in support of a proposition embodied in the aristocratic approach, and at another time cited in support of a proposition embodied in the democratic approach. This will occasion no confusion if it is recalled that *ideas, not men, are the objects of classification.* On the whole, it is true that those who adopt the major premise of one school tend to ignore the social processes central to the major premise of the other school. Yet there are some exceptions, particularly De Tocqueville, who analyzed not only the need for insulation of elites, but also the role played by multiple autonomous groups in the insulation of non-elites.

What follows is not an historical reconstruction of ideas on mass society, but a logical reconstruction of two major intellectual traditions that are intermingled in the literature on mass society. *Our integrated statement of mass-society theory is based on elements drawn from both traditions. At the same time, it accepts the democratic concern with the identification of conditions favorable to the preservation of democratic values.*

The Loss of Authority in Mass Society

During the nineteenth century, aristocratic critics of bourgeois society spun a rhetoric of pessimism concerning the value-standards men live by in an age of increasing materialism and equalitarianism. Le Bon crystallized this theme in sociological terms when he depicted the times as an "era of crowds," and spoke bitingly of crowds as vehicles in the downfall of civilization: "the populace is sovereign, and the tide of barbarism mounts" (1947, pp. 14, 207). Ortega popularized this thesis as the "revolt of the masses," a situation which leads to the "sovereignty of the unqualified" (1932, p. 25). Such present-day critics as T. S. Eliot (1948) use the term "mass society" in this pejorative sense to designate the alleged destructiveness of popular pressures on traditional values and elites.

Aristocratic theorists believe that liberty and equality are incompatible: "The spread of democratic equal rights facilitates, as Nietzsche prophesied, the equal violation of rights" (Viereck, 1955, p. 96). The paradigmatic experiences underlying this imagery were the French Revolution and the 1848 revolutions against the ancient regimes. The heart of the imagery itself is the *equalitarian society*, without excellence, distinction, style, meaning. Such a (mass) society is viewed as lacking the moral basis for resisting Caesarism, for preventing political tryanny as well as cultural decay.

Thus De Tocqueville has written:

I believe that it is easier to establish an absolute and despotic government among a people in which the conditions of society are equal than among any other; and I think that if such a government were once established among such a people, it not only would oppress men, but would eventually strip each of them of several of the highest qualities of humanity. (1945, v. II, p. 322)

Thus Burckhardt has written:

So long as the masses can bring pressure on their leaders, one value after another must be sacrificed: position, property, religion, distinguished tradition, higher learning. (Quoted by Viereck, 1956, p. 159)

Thus Mannheim has written:

The open character of democratic mass society, together with its

growth in size and the tendency towards general public participation, not only produces far too many elites but also deprives
these elites of the exclusiveness which they need [to perform
their functions]. . . . The lack of leadership in late liberal mass
society can . . . be . . . diagnosed as the result of the change for
the worse in selecting the elite. We must recognize further that
it is this general lack of direction in modern mass society that
gives the opportunity to groups with dictatorial ambitions.
(1940, pp. 86-7)

Thus Lippmann has written:

Where mass opinion dominates the government, there is a mor-
bid derangement of the true functions of power. The derangement brings about the enfeeblement, verging on paralysis, of the
capacity to govern. (1956, p. 19)

The conception of mass society contained in such writings as these includes three major terms: (a) growing
equalitarianism (loss of traditional authority); (b) widespread readiness to support anti-aristocratic forms of rule
(quest for popular authority); (c) rule by the masses
(domination by pseudo-authority). In this universe of discourse, "mass society" is the opposite of aristocratic order.
Mass society is the condition under which rule by the masses
—either directly or through the popularly supported dema-
goguc—displaces aristocratic rule. This condition is equality
of voice in the determination of social policy. Therefore,
mass society is the equalitarian society, in which the masses
seek to raise up leaders in their own image. As a result, it
produces rule by the incompetent.

However, the incompetence of the many is not what
distinguishes mass society, according to the aristocratic criticism. Mass society is new, whereas there always has been
widespread ignorance in society.[4] Mannheim observes in
this connection that the student of such changes as the loss
of distinctive art styles, the increasing intellectual inde-
cisiveness, or the decline of leadership, "if he is not used
to noticing the social mechanisms at work behind the im-

---

4. Thus Ortega remarks that mass society is "entirely new in the history
of our modern civilization" (1932, p. 21).

mediate concrete events is inclined to believe . . . that human beings are today less talented and less creative and have less initiative than in earlier periods" (1940, p. 87). What has changed is the structural relationship between the many and the few. In the mass society, there is a marked increase in opportunities for the many to intervene in areas previously reserved to the few. These opportunities invite the determination of social policies and cultural standards by large numbers who are not competent to make such decisions.

Mass society from this standpoint is the society in which there is a *loss of exclusiveness of elites*:[5] it is a social structure possessing high access to governing groups. High access to elites results from such procedures as direct popular elections and the shared expectation that public opinion is sovereign. When elites are easily accessible, the masses pressure them to conform to the transitory general will: "the voice of the masses [is] preponderant" (Le Bon, 1947, p. 15).[6] Therefore, loss of authority on the part of institutional elites results from widespread opportunities to participate in the formation of major social policies.

A system in which there is high access to elites generates popular pressures on the elites that prevent them from performing their creative and value-sustaining functions. People are not expected to have particular qualifications to make different kinds of decisions. Public opinion, viewed as the transitory general will, is regarded as the *immediate* as well as ultimate arbiter of all matters of policy and taste. Therefore, *anyone* is qualified; anyone may feel justified in judging or trying to influence any decision. As a result, the aristocratic critics claim, it is not simply that a large number of individuals is unqualified, but rather, it is the

5. The term "elite" as used in this study refers to a relatively small circle of people who claim and are charged with the responsibility for framing and sustaining fundamental values and policies in their area of competence. See below, pp. 51 ff., for further remarks on our use of the term.

6. Ortega also speaks of "the predominance . . . of the mass" (1932, p. 16).

very *system* that is unqualified. For the system makes no provision for separating the qualified from the unqualified; and therefore excellence (whether in governing, in art, or in any other sphere) can neither be discovered, developed, nor protected.[7] It is a situation in which elites cannot be creative nor can they deeply influence society. But only elites can perform these functions: "Civilizations as yet have only been created and directed by a small intellectual aristocracy, never by crowds. Crowds are only powerful for destruction" (Le Bon, 1947, p. 18).

Insofar as popular participation cannot be controlled, it destroys liberty as well as authority. Equalitarianism is judged to be incompatible with individual liberty, for "liberty is preserved not by mass-will nor by counting noses but by tiny, heroic natural-aristocracies and by the majesty —beyond mob majorities—of moral law" (Viereck, 1955, p. 104).

But is it the mere quantitative fact of widespread participation in the setting of social policy which destroys elite functions and thereby liberty? Aristocratic critics would not deny that if people intervened only at certain points in the decision-making process, and in a manner regulated and controlled according to set rules, then elites would be protected from undue interference and could fulfill their critical functions. They assume, however, that popular participation will not be of this kind. Thus Le Bon (1947) uses such terms as suggestible, unconscious, impulsive, capricious, and the like, to characterize popular participation where elites are accessible. And Ortega (1932) speaks of the indocility of the masses in a similar vein. These aristocratic critics are arguing that when people intervene in decision-making processes in an excitable and intractable manner, liberty is threatened.

We must ask the aristocratic critics how *equality* of opportunity to participate leads to *unrestrained* intervention, as in political strikes. We may agree that high

---

7. Cf. Selznick (1952, p. 278) and Mannheim (1940, pp. 82 ff.).

access to elites is a permissive condition for recurrent mass behavior of this sort. But it is not a sufficient condition, since *non-elites may be restrained on their side, by means of their own groups and values.* That is, those members of society who identify themselves with the central values of a constitutional order are not likely to exploit opportunities to subvert elites. On the other hand, people who are *alienated* from society may express their resentment by using the most accessible instruments of action to impose their will. In short, the source of mass behavior cannot be located *only* in the structure of elites. It also must be found in the structure of non-elites, in a set of conditions close to the personal environment of the people who engage in mass behavior. Open elites can provide the "pull" for unrestrained participation in the vital centers of society, but not the "push." Since the democratic criticism specifies a set of conditions under which people will be propelled into mass actions, the aristocratic view of mass society may be strengthened by taking these additional conditions into account.[8]

The Loss of Community
in Mass Society

From the democratic viewpoint, the threat posed by mass society is less how elites may be protected from the masses and more how non-elites may be shielded from domination by elites. This difference is part of the larger difference dividing the two approaches: concern with oppor-

---

8. Several aristocratic thinkers also have been concerned with this problem, and have influenced the formulations of later democratic theorists. But it has remained for the latter to provide a basic understanding of sources of mass behavior in the transformation of community. Thus, a present-day conservative thinker has written: "I think that one of the principal errors of conservatively-inclined men has been their neglect of the need for true community" (Kirk, 1956, p. 129).

tunities for and functions of the few, on the one hand, versus concern with widespread opportunities for large numbers of people to participate in the collective life, on the other hand. The aristocratic position judges the formulation of broad social policy to be the responsibility and capability of the few, whereas the democratic position implies that potentially all members of society share in this responsibility.

Aristocratic critics attribute loss of liberty to the rise of popular participation in areas previously limited to the specially qualified: mass society is a condition under which there is too much control by the many over the few. Democratic critics, in their turn, attribute loss of liberty to the rise of mass manipulation and mobilization in areas previously left to the privacy of the individual and the group: mass society is a condition under which there is too much control by the few over the many. In short, one conception views mass society as unlimited democracy ("hyperdemocracy" in Ortega's terms), the other as unlimited tyranny.

Now, of course, these two states could be intimately related. In fact, one student of the problem has stated the belief that "a whole literature on mass behavior and mass psychology [has] demonstrated and popularized the wisdom, so familiar to the ancients, of the affinity between democracy and dictatorship, between mob rule and tyranny" (Arendt, 1951, pp. 309-10). It is the thesis of this study that such an affinity is caught by the concept of mass society; but the fact remains that unlimited democracy is not unlimited tyranny, even though it may become so. Therefore, it remains to be clarified how a theory of mass society may specify this relationship.

Another difference between the two approaches to mass society concerns the consequences of equalitarianism. The democratic criticism does not find equality of condition inherently inimical to liberty, nor does it look only to elites for the defense of liberty. From this point of view, the chief characteristic of the mass is not brutality and backwardness, as the aristocratic criticism implies, but isolation and amorphous social relations. Furthermore, *mass behavior may characterize people in high status positions as well as those from lower classes;* "highly cultured people were particularly attracted to mass movements [in post-war Europe]" (Arendt, 1951, p. 310).

What concerns the democratic critics is the possible emergence of another elite modeled after those thrown up by the Nazi and Bolshevik revolutions, with the consequent destruction of political democracy. The core of this imagery is the *atomized society.* Mass society is a situation in which an aggregate of individuals are related to one another only by way of their relation to a common authority, especially the state. That is, individuals are not directly related to one another in a variety of independent groups. A population in this condition is not insulated in any way from the ruling group, nor yet from elements within itself. For insulation requires a multiplicity of independent and often conflicting forms of association, each of which is strong enough to ward off threats to the autonomy of the individual. But it is precisely the weakness or absence of such social groups, *rather than their equality,* which distinguishes the mass society, according to these theorists. In their absence, people lack the resources to restrain their own behavior as well as that of others. Social atomization engenders strong feelings of alienation and anxiety, and therefore the disposition to engage in extreme behavior to escape from these tensions. In a mass society there is a heightened readiness to form hyper-attachments to symbols and leaders. "Such loyalty can be expected only from the completely isolated human being who, without any other social ties . . . derives his sense of having a place in the world only from his belonging to a movement" (Arendt, 1951, pp. 316-17). Total loyalty, in turn, is the psychological basis for total domination, i.e., totalitarianism.

There are three major terms implied in the democratic

criticism of mass society: (a) growing atomization (loss of community); (b) widespread readiness to embrace new ideologies (quest for community); (c) totalitarianism (total domination by pseudo-community). In this universe of discourse, mass society is a condition in which elite domination replaces democratic rule. Mass society is objectively the *atomized* society, and subjectively the *alienated* population. Therefore, mass society is a system in which there is *high availability of a population for mobilization by elites.*

People become available for mobilization by elites when they lack or lose an independent group life. The term *masses* applies "only where we deal with people who . . . cannot be integrated into any organization based on common interest, into political parties or municipal governments or professional organizations or trade unions" (Arendt, 1951, p. 305). The lack of autonomous relations generates widespread social alienation. Alienation heightens responsiveness to the appeal of mass movements because they provide occasions for expressing resentment against what is, as well as promises of a totally different world. In short, *people who are atomized readily become mobilized.* Since totalitarianism is a state of total mobilization, mass society is highly vulnerable to totalitarian movements and regimes.

We must ask the democratic critics at this point whether mass society is totalitarian, or only may become so. Democratic critics tend to construe totalitarianism as mass society, because elite domination based on a mobilized population is the central meaning of their conception of totalitarianism. However, they also tend to designate societies that are vulnerable to totalitarianism as mass society. For example, both Weimar Germany and Nazi Germany have been called mass societies. This obscures the problem of developmental patterns, since factors which encourage totalitarian movements in political democracies are not necessarily the same as those which *sustain* totalitarian regimes once they are in power.

It is necessary, therefore, to distinguish between a mass society and a totalitarian society.

We must next inquire whether an available population constitutes by itself a condition sufficient to result in numerous mass movements, as the democratic theorists imply. There are at least three reasons why high access to elites must also be present. In the first place, it is apparent that in order for available masses to become mobilized at all, agents of mobilization—for example, Communist spokesmen and organizations—must have opportunities to contact and appeal to large numbers of people. This requires readily accessible channels of communication. Moreover, if the paths to power were not open, there would be little incentive to mobilize and incite masses. In this sense, an accessible elite can serve as a magnet, both to would-be totalitarian leaders and to discontented masses. People in the mass (i.e., an undifferentiated and amorphous collectivity) are highly susceptible to total mobilization; but unless there is access to the means of communication and power, counterelites (such as Communist leaders) will not be able to seize the opportunity provided by the mass for the conquest of total power.

Secondly, the success of totalitarian movements is contingent upon the vulnerability of existing elites. An accessible elite should not be equated with a vulnerable elite, for the strength or weakness of elites depends upon a host of factors other than their degree of accessibility. Nevertheless, an accessible elite is more vulnerable than one which is not accessible, other things being equal. When access is low, elites are relatively immune to popular pressures, so that mass movements peter out without overturning elites or infiltrating elite positions. Accessible elites more easily succumb to the attacks of totalitarian movements.

There is yet a third reason for suggesting that an available population does not automatically call forth elite domination. Totalitarian regimes are installed by new elites who have successfully mobilized an available population. But if this were in fact the sole condition required for the seizure of total power by new elites, how is it that the old elites, favored by this very same condition (i.e., an atomized population available for mobilization), have not themselves absorbed total power? Evidently *elites may be restrained on their side by means of their own relations and values.* Old elites generally lack the will and capacity to mobilize a large population. The one major exception is when the very existence of the social order is believed to be threatened, as in war or revolution. That is, mobilized movements led by representatives of existing institutions tend to be military ventures against external or internal enemies. Such mass movements may be developed in response to the mobilization of forces by another nation or by a revolutionary group, or in response to the expectation of such an enemy mobilization. It is under these conditions that a mass society may move toward totalitarianism under the direction of institutional rather than anti-institutional leadership. The model of the "garrison state" (Lasswell, 1941) is precisely such a state of mobilization by established elites in the name of national security.

The "garrison state" undoubtedly is a possible course along which mass society can move. But there are a number of factors which militate against mobilization of large numbers by existing elites (except under conditions of total war). In the first place, these elites are part of a going concern, and this alone makes for an essentially mundane orientation. Activism entails a readiness to reject routine modes of activity, and therefore tends to be eschewed by groups whose very power is bound to established routines. It usually requires a new elite devoid of the restraints incident upon institutional participation to mobilize widespread activism. As a form of charismatic leadership, the totalitarian elite is "outside the realm of everyday routine" and is "foreign to all rules" (Weber, 1947, p. 361).

Another reason why existing elites infrequently set in motion a large population is the presence of leadership rivalries. These conflicts between leaders operate as checks on the power of each, including any attempts to expand power by mobilizing masses.

In addition, existing elites may be restrained by their value commitments. They ordinarily have a strong stake in preserving the social order, for their own positions are legitimated by established values. Those who are successful are often more amenable to abiding by the rules of the game. Further, the achievement of high position may reflect or induce a heightened sense of responsibility for and awareness of institutional values.

Thus it is that popular mobilization generally is the work of counter-elites, since they are not inhibited by commitments to the social order, nor by constraints resulting from participation in a balance of power.[9] These counter-elites are pushed towards making allies among the masses, since this is the only way to gain total power in mass society. Finally, established elites in a mass society not only lack the capacity to mobilize a large population; they also are ill-equipped to protect their organizations from penetration by counter-elites bent on destroying an existing order. This point will be developed in detail when we analyze the origins of mass movements in Part II.

We may therefore conclude that high vulnerability to the *development* of totalitarianism presupposes accessible elites as well as available non-elites. A rising totalitarian movement finds its prey not only in an exposed mass but

---

9. A recent review of the literature on community conflict in the United States (Coleman, 1957, p. 13) notes that "both community organizations and community leaders are faced with constraints when a dispute arises; the formation of a combat group to carry on the controversy and the emergence of a previous unknown as the combat leader are in part results of the *immobility of responsible organizations and leaders.* Both the new leader and the new organization are freed from some of the usual shackles of community norms and internal cross-pressures which make pre-existing organizations and leaders tend to soften the dispute."

also in an exposed elite. The penetration of an existing elite by a successful totalitarian movement (as the Nazis penetrated the Weimar government) is *prima facie* evidence of its accessibility. On the other hand, the maintenance of a population in a state of mobilization by a given (totalitarian) elite requires low access to elites; otherwise the ruling group would not be able to maintain its power.

Thus, the concept of mass society, in order to be useful for a theory of the transformation of democratic into totalitarian society, *necessarily* presupposes accessible elites. *The democratic criticism of mass society requires for its completion the notion of accessible elites provided by aristocratic critics.* It now may be shown that the negative consequences of accessible elites envisioned by aristocratic critics are greatly increased when non-elites are available by virtue of the loss of community.

Aristocratic theorists assume that whenever people are given the opportunity to participate in the shaping of social policies, they will do so in a destructive manner. But the opportunity for widespread participation in society does not automatically call forth mass action unrestrained by social relations and cultural norms. Not all members of a society, but only *people in the mass* are disposed to seize the opportunity provided by accessible elites to impress mass standards on all spheres of society, and to do so in an unrestrained manner. This is true for two reasons. First, when large numbers of people are interrelated only as members of a mass, they are more likely to pressure elites to provide satisfactions previously supplied by a plurality of more proximate groups. Second, they are likely to do so in a direct and unmediated way, because there is a paucity of intervening groups to channelize and filter popular participation in the larger society. As a result, mass participation tends to be irrational and unrestrained, since there are few points at which it may be checked by personal experience and the experience of others. Where people are not securely related to a plurality of independent groups, they are available for all kinds of adventures and "activist modes of intervention" in the larger society. It is one thing for a population to participate at specified times and in institutional ways for defined interests—for example, through trade associations and trade unions, or in elections. It is quite another to create *ad hoc* methods of direct pressure on critical centers of society, such as the "invasion" of a state legislature, street political gangs, etc. (Selznick, 1952, p. 294). It is the latter form of collective activity that the aristocratic theorists fear, but they err in assuming that equal access to elites is sufficient to produce it: widespread availability attendant upon social atomization also must exist.

Thus, each conception of mass society requires the other for its completion. Together they provide the basis for a general theory of mass society.

Chapter 2

Conditions
of Mass Society

THE ARISTOCRATIC critique of mass society yields the idea
of accessible elites, and the democratic critique yields the
idea of available non-elites. We have shown that the consequences imputed to each are more likely to follow from
a combination of both factors than from either one alone.
This suggests a more general conception of mass society
than that contained in the aristocratic or democratic version. *Mass society is a social system in which elites are readily
accessible to influence by non-elites and non-elites are readily
available for mobilization by elites.*

This conception of mass society may be better understood by comparing it with other types of societies. For this
purpose, we shall consider communal society, pluralist society, and totalitarian society, insofar as they can be characterized by other combinations of the two variables of (a)
accessibility of elites and (b) availability of non-elites.
Access and availability vary in kind as well as in degree.
For example, access to elites may be institutionalized or
it may be direct; access can take the form of membership
in elites or of selection of elites. These are some of the main
kinds of access. There are important differences between
social systems in respect to the kinds of access to elites (or
the kinds of availability of non-elites) that predominate in

each; this aspect of the problem will be explored subsequently. For the moment, we are concerned only with the *degree* of access and availability. As a rough indicator of the degree of access to elites we shall use the extent to which members of the society participate in the selection of elites, and as a comparable measure of the degree of availability of non-elites we may use the extent to which members of the society lack attachments to independent groups. Of each type of society we shall now ask only whether it involves high or low access to elites, high or low availability of non-elites.

		AVAILABILITY OF NON-ELITES	
		Low	High
ACCESSIBILITY OF ELITES	Low	communal society	totalitarian society
	High	pluralist society	mass society

Communal society requires inaccessible elites and unavailable non-elites if it is to sustain its traditional structure —as in certain medieval communities. Elites are inaccessible in that elite elements and standards are selected and fixed by traditional ascription. Non-elites are unavailable in that people are firmly bound by kinship and community. Such a population is very difficult to mobilize unless powerful forces have eroded communal ties, as happened in the Late Middle Ages, when the incipient processes of urbanization and industrialization began their destruction of the medieval community, thereby unloosing portions of the population for participation in the various millennial movements that flourished during this period.

Pluralist society requires accessible elites and unavailable non-elites if it is to sustain its freedom and diversity—as in certain liberal democracies. Elites are accessible in that competition among independent groups opens many channels of communication and power. The population is unavailable in that people possess multiple commitments to diverse and autonomous groups. The mobilization of a population bound by multiple commitments would require the breaking up of large numbers of independent organizations, as totalitarian movements have sought to do.

Mass society requires both accessible elites and available non-elites if it is to exhibit a high rate of mass behavior. Elites are accessible and non-elites are available in that there is a paucity of independent groups between the state and the family to protect either elites or non-elites from manipulation and mobilization by the other. In the absence of social autonomy at all levels of society, large numbers of people are pushed and pulled toward activist modes of intervention in vital centers of society; and mass-oriented leaders have the opportunity to mobilize this activism for the capture of power. As a result, freedom is precarious in mass society.

Totalitarian society requires an inaccessible elite and an available population if it is to sustain a system of total control from above—as in certain modern dictatorships. The elite is inaccessible in that elite elements are selected and fixed through co-optation, by virtue of a monopoly over the means of coercion and persuasion in the hands of those at the apex of the structure. The population is available in that its members lack all those independent social formations that could serve as a basis of resistance to the elite. Instead, the population is mobilized by the elite through multiple organizations taken over or created for that purpose.

These are abstract types of society; no large-scale society is purely communal, pluralist, mass, or totalitarian. However, any given society would appear to be like one type more than like other types. For example, large, complex societies always contain some pluralist elements, so that total control is impossible, even under totalitarian regimes. Yet some societies give much greater weight to pluralist elements than do others. They not only exhibit a much greater degree of institutional autonomy, but in addition, "it is acknowledged and guaranteed and finds support in the legal system, the ethos and the distribution of legitimate power" (Shils, 1956, p. 154).

A weakness of the two theories of mass society may be identified in light of the model of four types of society. Aristocratic critics fasten on popular access to elites as the distinguishing characteristic of mass society, and thereby confound pluralist society with mass society.[10] Democratic critics, on the other hand, fasten on the availability of atomized non-elites in their conception of mass society, and thereby confound totalitarian society with mass society.[11] By distinguishing mass society from totalitarian society, on the one side, and pluralist society, on the other, the model presented here would appear to be a more fruitful one for the examina-

---

10. Thus Lippmann (1956, p. 50) judges all democratic republics to be mass-dominated by virtue of their accessible elites: "It is significant, I think, certainly it is at least suggestive, that while nearly all the Western governments have been in deep trouble since the First World War, the constitutional monarchies of Scandinavia, the Low Countries, and the United Kingdom have shown greater capacity to endure, to preserve order with freedom, than the republics of France, Germany, Spain and Italy. . . . The evaporation of the imponderable powers, a total dependence upon the assemblies and the mass electorates, has upset the balance of powers between the two functions of the state. The executive has lost both its material and its ethereal powers. The assemblies and the mass electorates have acquired the monopoly of effective powers."

11. Thus Mills states that all modern societies, including both democratic societies (especially the United States) and totalitarian societies (especially the Soviet Union), are "mass societies" in that they allegedly feature elite domination of atomized masses (1956, p. 310): "In all modern societies, the autonomous associations standing between the various classes and the state tend to lose their effectiveness as vehicles of reasoned opinion and instruments for the rational exertion of political will. Such associations can be deliberately broken up and thus turned into passive instruments of rule, or they can more slowly wither away from lack of use in the face of centralized means of power. But whether they are destroyed in a week, or wither in a generation, such associations are replaced in virtually every sphere of life by centralized organizations, and it is such organizations with all their new means of power that take charge of the terrorized or—as the case may be—merely intimidated, society of masses." (See also ibid., p. 27.)

tion of problems related to social structure and freedom.[12]

Our conception of mass society involves the following major proposition: *a high rate of mass behavior may be expected when both elites and non-elites lack social insulation; that is, when elites are accessible to direct intervention by non-elites, and when non-elites are available for direct mobilization by elites.*

We shall consider the three terms of this proposition: (1) mass behavior, (2) accessible elites, (3) available non-elites.

Mass Behavior

Mass behavior is a form of collective behavior exhibiting the following characteristics.[13] (a) *The focus of attention is remote from personal experience and daily life.* Remote objects are national and international issues or events, abstract symbols, and whatever else is known only through the mass media. Of course, not *any* concern for remote objects is a manifestation of mass behavior. Only when that concern leads to direct and activist modes of response can we speak of mass behavior. However, merely by virtue of the fact that mass behavior always involves remote objects certain consequences are likely to follow. Concern for remote objects tends to lack the definiteness, independence, sense of reality,

12. DeGré also distinguishes between these three types of social systems. His distinction between totalitarian society and mass society closely parallels our own (1946, pp. 528-9) : "Totalitarian society . . . has systematically destroyed all independent groups and autonomous opinion. It resembles the atomistic [i.e., mass] society in that the individual again operates without the backing of any group of his own. It differs from the atomistic [i.e., mass] society, however, in the fact that this time the atomized individual faces the full power of an omnipotent Leviathan state."

13. Our conception of mass behavior borrows from Blumer (1946, pp. 185 ff.) and Selznick (1952, pp. 281-97) . However, it departs from both in several respects. Reiwald (1949) provides an extensive review of the literature on mass behavior and related phenomena.

and responsibility to be found in concern for proximate objects. The sphere of proximate objects consists of things that directly concern the individual:

his family, his business dealings, his hobbies, his friends and enemies, his township or ward, his class, church, trade union or any other social group of which he is an active member—the things under his personal observation, the things which are familiar to him independently of what his newspaper tells him, which he can directly influence or manage and for which he develops the kind of responsibility that is induced by a direct relation to the favorable or unfavorable effects of a course of action. (Schumpeter, 1947, pp. 258-9)

The sense of reality and responsibility declines as the object of concern becomes more remote:

Now this comparative definiteness of volition and rationality of behavior does not suddenly vanish as we move away from those concerns of daily life in the home and in business which educate and discipline us. In the realm of public affairs there are sectors that are more within the reach of the citizen's mind than others. This is true, first, of local affairs. Even there we find a reduced power of discerning facts, a reduced preparedness to act upon them, a reduced sense of responsibility. . . . Second, there are many national issues that concern individuals and groups so directly and unmistakably as to evoke volitions that are genuine and definite enough. The most important instance is afforded by issues involving immediate and personal pecuniary profit to individual voters and groups of voters. . . . However, when we move still farther away from the private concerns of the family and the business office into those regions of national and international affairs that lack a direct and unmistakable link with those private concerns, individual volition, command of facts and method of inference soon [decline]. (Schumpeter, 1947, pp. 260-1)

(b) *The mode of response to remote objects is direct.* The lessening of the sense of reality and responsibility and effective volition with the greater remoteness of the focus of attention has particularly marked consequences when the mode of response is direct, rather than being mediated by several intervening layers of social relations. People act directly when they do not engage in discussion on the matter at hand, and when they do not act through groups in which they are capable of persuading and being persuaded by their fellows.

At times, people may act directly by grasping those means of action which lie immediately to hand. They may employ various more or less coercive measures against those individuals and groups who resist them (Heberle, 1951, p. 378). For example, when large numbers of people feel that taxes are intolerably high, they may engage in quite different types of action. On the one hand, they may seek to change the tax laws by financing lobbyists, electing representatives, persuading others of their views by means of discussion, and so forth. These types of action are mediated by institutional relations, and are therefore subject to rules concerning legitimate modes of political action. On the other hand, people may seek to prevent others from paying their taxes and forcibly impede officials from collecting taxes, as in the instance of the Poujadists in France. This is direct action.

Mass behavior is associated with activist interpretations of democracy and with increasing reliance on force to resolve social conflict. . . . The breakdown of normal restraints, including internalized standards of right conduct, and established channels of action . . . frees the mass to engage in direct, unmediated efforts to achieve its goals and to lay hands upon the most readily accessible instruments of action. Ordinarily, even in countries having democratic constitutional systems, the population is so structured as to inhibit direct access to the agencies of decision. The electorate participates at specified times and in defined ways; it is not free to create *ad hoc* methods of pressure. The citizen, even when organized in a pressure group supporting, say, a farm lobby, can vote, write letters, visit his congressman, withhold funds, and engage in similar respectable actions. Other forms of activity are strange to him. But when this code has lost its power over him, he will become available for activist modes of intervention. (Selznick, 1952, pp. 293-4)

Political activism tends to be undemocratic because it abrogates institutional procedures intended to guarantee both majority choice and minority rights, and denies respect for principles of free competition and public discussion as the bases for compromising conflicting interests. When political activism is taken to the extreme, it is expressed in violence against opposition. This violence may be restricted to sporadic riots and mob action; or it may become embodied in the very principles of a mass movement. A philosophy of direct action was developed by Sorel (1950) in his idea of the general strike, an idea which influenced such mass movements as revolutionary syndicalism in France, as well as many totalitarian movements, such as fascism in Italy, nazism in Germany, and communism in Russia (Heberle, 1951, pp. 382-6). Totalitarian movements carry their activism to extremes, as indicated by the widespread use of violence on the part of the Fascists in post-war Italy, the Nazis in the Weimar Republic, and the Communists in all countries in which they have developed organizations. Violence also characterizes certain mass movements, like the I.W.W. and the K.K.K. Violence in word and deed is the hallmark of the mass movement uncommitted to institutional means. Mass behavior, then, involves direct, activist modes of response to remote symbols.

(c) Mass behavior also tends to be highly unstable, readily shifting its focus of attention and intensity of response. Activist responses are likely to alternate with apathetic responses. *Mass apathy* as well as mass activism is widespread in mass society. Mass apathy, like mass activism, is unstable and unpredictable, since it, too, is born of social alienation; and as an expression of resentment against the social order it can be transformed into extremist attacks on that order in times of crisis. In these respects, mass apathy differs from that indifference to public matters that is based on traditional conceptions of appropriate spheres of participation (for example, the indifference of women who believe that politics is a man's affair).

(d) When mass behavior becomes organized around a program and acquires a certain continuity in purpose and effort, it takes on the character of a *mass movement* (Blumer, 1946, p. 187). Mass movements generally have the following characteristics: their objectives are remote and extreme; they favor activist modes of intervention in the social order; they mobilize uprooted and atomized sections of the population; they lack an internal structure of independent groups (such as regional or functional units with some freedom of action). Totalitarian movements also possess these characteristics, but mass movements need not become totalitarian. The distinctive character of totalitarian movements lies in their effort to gain total control over their followers and over the whole society. Totalitarian movements are highly organized by an elite bent on total power, whereas mass movements tend to be amorphous collectivities, often without any stable leadership. The difference between the Communist movement and the I.W.W. is an example of the difference between a totalitarian movement and a mass movement.

Mass movements are miniature mass societies; totalitarian movements are miniature totalitarian societies. This parallelism implies the major similarity and the major difference between the two types of social movements: they both are based on atomized masses rather than on independent social groups, as are mass societies and totalitarian societies; on the other hand, the amorphous structure of the mass movement corresponds to the ease of access to elites in mass society, while the cadre organization of the totalitarian movement corresponds to the inaccessibility of the elite in totalitarian society.

Mass movements offer excellent opportunities for penetration by totalitarian groups. The Communist party, for example, deliberately creates cadres for the purpose of capturing mass movements.

The Communist membership functions as the cadre of a wider mass movement. Each member has special training and ideally should be able to lead nonparty groups as they may from time to time become accessible. . . . In sum, the cadre party is a highly manipulable skeleton organization of trained agents; it is sustained by political combat and is linked to the mass movement as its members become leaders of wider groups in the community. (Selznick, 1952, p. 18)

Examples of mass movements which have been penetrated by the Communist party with varying success include anarchist and syndicalist movements in France, Italy, and Spain.[14]

Since totalitarian movements typically are mass movements which have been captured by totalitarian cadres, we shall refer to totalitarian movements as "mass movements" in the present study when we wish to emphasize the contention that totalitarian movements are organizations of masses. This is not a matter of definition, but requires theoretical and empirical support. For there is a widely-held theory that communism and fascism (the major cases of totalitarian movements) are essentially *class* movements, that is, expressions of specific class interests and forms of class organization bent on furthering these interests. It undoubtedly is true that not only some theorists but also many individual citizens (for example, in France) think in these class terms, and in the latter case express this belief by voting for a Communist (or Fascist) slate. The burden of the present study, however, is that large numbers of people do not respond to totalitarian movements primarily from the standpoint of economic calculus; but instead, they respond to the nihilistic tone of totalitarian movements, as an expression of their feelings of resentment against the present and hope for something completely new in the future. In Part III, we shall

---

14. See pp. 155-56 below, for a discussion of these cases.

adduce considerable evidence to show that the strongest response to the totalitarian appeal is *not* to be found among those who are involved in class organization and class struggle; on the contrary, the strongest response comes from people with the weakest attachment to class organizations, or any other kind of social group. A totalitarian movement attracts socially isolated members of *all* classes. Furthermore, whenever totalitarian groups gain power, they seek to smash all class organizations and to suppress all class interests. The inference is that movements which repeatedly have shown their contempt for class interests they are sometimes alleged to embody (and themselves sometimes claim to represent) can hardly be said to make their primary appeal to class interests.[15]

What class analysis does not help to explain is the *extremism* of totalitarian movements: their appeal to the most extreme dispositions of individuals and their readiness to go to any extreme in the pursuit of their objectives. But it is precisely this quality of extremism which makes these movements so threatening to democratic politics and individual liberty.

The extremist must be deeply alienated from the complex of rules which keep the strivings for various values in restraint and balance. An extremist group is an alienated group. This means that it is fundamentally hostile to the political order. It cannot share that sense of affinity to persons or the attachment to the institutions which confine political conflicts to peaceful solutions. Its hostility is incompatible with that freedom from in-

---

15. If we were trying to tell the whole story of why people support totalitarian movements, we would have to differentiate between leaders, active members, inactive members, voters, etc.—since reasons for adherence are associated with extent of involvement in a movement. Since the present study is primarily concerned with the *popular* response to totalitarian movements (as indicated, for example, by the number of votes totalitarian parties gain), differences like those which obtain between leaders and members of these movements are not very relevant. For a study which shows differences of this order, see Almond (1954) .

tense emotion which pluralistic politics needs for its prosperity. (Shils, 1956, p. 231)

The present study is concerned with the fate of democracy insofar as it is affected by the opportunities provided for the growth of mass movements; and it seeks to analyze these opportunities with the aid of concepts of mass society.

Mass society is characterized by an abundance of mass movements. Other types of society are characterized by different kinds of social movements. Social movements which arise within communal society are characteristically traditional movements. For example, revival movements tend to be tradition-oriented, and manifest many of the features of the communal society within which they arise. Social movements which develop within pluralist societies are typically reform movements. For example, labor movements are reform movements when they seek to change only limited and specific aspects of working conditions, by developing a public opinion favorable to their aims in a constitutional manner. In totalitarian society, there is only one effective movement, and that is the totalitarian movement which supports the regime.

Mass movements may arise in non-mass societies, although they are not frequent in these societies. For example, millennial movements with mass characteristics arose at least as early as the Middle Ages. Mannheim has fixed the beginning of movements which combine the idea of a millennial kingdom on earth with the activism of large numbers of people in the "orgiastic chiliasm" of the Anabaptists: "the 'spiritualization of politics' . . . may be said to have begun at this turn in history" (1936, p. 191). The appearance of outbursts of social chiliasm in the Middle Ages should not obscure the fact that they were only sporadic occurrences which, though they may have engendered new sects, generally did not transform major institutions (Talmon, 1952, p. 9).

Mass behavior occurs at a low rate and in peripheral spheres in communal society, because the inaccessibility of elites inhibits mass behavior from above and the unavailability of non-elites inhibits it from below. In pluralist society, mass behavior also is located in peripheral areas, but the rate is higher because there are more remote symbols clamoring for attention (due to the accessibility of channels of communication). In totalitarian society, the great power of the elite suppresses spontaneous behavior of masses, but that mass behavior that does occur tends to impinge on the vital centers of society (witness the rarity but the explosiveness of spontaneous mass actions in totalitarian societies, such as those which took place in East Berlin, Potsdam, and Budapest). In mass society, mass behavior occurs at a high rate and in central spheres of society; mass behavior is inhibited neither from above nor from below because mass society possesses both accessible elites and available non-elites.

Accessible Elites

The term "elite" is used to refer to those *positions* in a social structure which are superordinate, such that the incumbents claim and are granted social superiority. The term also is used to refer to the *functions* attached to such positions, especially the special responsibility to form and defend value-standards in a certain social sphere. Now it is possible to have influence of this kind without possessing prestige. And it also happens that incumbents of high position may lack the special power or responsibility to set standards. But the close relationship between status and function in the sense indicated allows us to use the single term "elite" to refer to the combination of high position and special responsibility. An elite, then, is composed of people who by virtue of their social position have special responsibility for standards in a given social context.[16]

16. Cf. Selznick (1957, p. 120).

Since in any large and complex system the protection of standards necessarily must be the primary work of a relatively few people who possess the requisite values and skills, elites are indispensable to democratic as well as non-democratic groups. The question is, who may gain entrance into elites and who may influence them. In democratic groups there is widespread opportunity to enter elites and to influence them, whereas in non-democratic groups only the few have access.

Ease of entrance into elites and ease of influence over them (especially via selection of elites) are not the same thing, and may not even vary together. The measurement of access by comparing the social composition of elites with the social composition of non-elites (i.e., the community at large) uses only ease of entrance as a criterion. Similarly, comparison of the social composition of elites at different times is concerned only with this aspect of access.[17]

Access to membership in elites has been increasing in all modern societies. There has been a shift in the basic principles for entering elites in a direction consonant with the requirements of industrial organization. As feudal society gave way to modern society, the principle governing entrance into elites changed from recruitment based on blood to recruitment based on wealth. With the further development of modern industry, achievement increasingly has come to prevail as the major means for entering elites. As this is true for totalitarian as well as democratic industrial societies, it is evident that the criteria for entering elites may not be used alone to measure access to elites.

Since the central meaning of access is that of the non-elite's influence on elite conduct, representative social composition of elites is not a dependable basis for inferring the extent to which elites are open or closed. A formally representative elite may constitute a closed system in which the

---

17. For example, Lasswell *et al.* (1952) treat only this aspect of access to elites. Mills (1956) also gives primary consideration to access to membership in elites, to the relative neglect of access to influence on elites.

members recruited from the various social strata are subsequently separated from the groups from which they came and are absorbed into a group with different (and often conflicting) standards and interests. From the standpoint of an elite, representative recruitment may be merely one way of taking into account the interests and values of non-elites, and it may be sufficient for an elite bent on its own exclusiveness to do only that much in order to free itself from more thorough-going dependence on non-elites.

By access we mean the sum total of all ways in which non-elites impinge on elites, and the net effect of these influences on the conduct of elites. Therefore, we need to have at least one other criterion of access besides ease of entrance, namely, some measure of the ease with which elites may be influenced from the outside.[18] One important measure of outside influence is the extent to which non-elites participate in the *selection* of elites; presumably the greater the role of a given non-elite in the determination of elite membership, the greater the weight elites grant to the anticipated reaction of the non-elite in their decisions. The composition of the selectors is a better measure of the accessibility of elites than is the composition of those who are selected.

Increasing access to political elites in Western countries generally has involved increasing participation by the middle and working classes in the selection of the elites prior to their achievement of membership in these governing groups. For example, working-class suffrage in England (greatly expanded in 1867) preceded the representation of workers in the English cabinet (which first occurred in 1906). The reverse situation, where equality of opportunity to enter political elites increases more rapidly than equality of opportunity to select the members of these elites, tends to occur when there is a sharp and sudden break with the established order, as is attested by the careers of many Jacobin and

---

18. For an extended discussion of access in the sense of differential opportunities to influence key points of decision, see Truman (1951, pp. 264-70 and *passim*).

Bolshevik revolutionaries. In these cases, persons of lower social origins had a markedly greater chance to become members of governing groups, while at the same time the chance for the individual citizen to participate in the selection of the rulers increased more slowly, or even decreased. In general, effective access to elites depends more on the opportunity to influence the selection of members of elites than on the opportunity to enter elites. Thus Marx is reported to have observed that "if open access to privileged position would be the only test for the degree of democratization of a society, the Society of Jesus would have to be considered a most democratic institution" (Coser, 1954, p. 239).

It is apparent that one may speak of more or less access to elites in the cultural as well as political spheres. This is what Mannheim implies in his conception of "the fundamental democratization" of society, which he saw as affecting the mode of elite formation in the intellectual, religious, and cultural, as well as political, spheres (1940, pp. 85 ff.). However, there is a problem in identifying the members of cultural, as over against political, elites. Whereas it is plausible to begin with the set of established positions of authority in major political institutions in order to locate political elites, this is a less efficacious method in the case of cultural elites. Editorial and publishing posts, or leading offices in radio, television, and cinema, provide their incumbents with real influence in shaping cultural values. But at least as significant as molders of culture are the major artists and writers of the day, the free-lance intellectuals whose positions as cultural leaders do not exist apart from their personal reputations. Therefore, there exists a certain ambiguity in what we mean by access to cultural elites.

Nevertheless, it is clear that in Western democracies there is increasing opportunity to select cultural leaders and models (for example, art styles) through the mass market, and a corresponding decline in the older system of class sponsorship (as in art patronage). There has been a "delegation of taste to majority suffrage" (Fiedler, 1955, p. 18), expressed through popular purchasing power. There also has been an increasing opportunity for people to become cultural leaders, through free education and open competition, and a decline in the importance of blood and property for the attainment of cultural leadership.

In order to determine long-run tendencies in access to elites, cultural as well as political, it may be sufficient to discover the proportion of the community which is formally free to participate in the selection of elites. But this measure proves inadequate once everyone may participate, as, for example, when universal suffrage becomes an established institution. Now we need more sensitive indicators which can take account of the *effectiveness* as well as the legitimacy of popular participation. For one thing, there must be *alternative choices* before popular participation can be other than the ritualistic incantation that "elections" are in totalitarian nations. For another, there must be *open channels of communication* before popular participation can be other than the manipulated vote that "elections" are in certain formally democratic associations (such as certain trade unions). *Access requires competition among elites,* for only in this manner can there be guaranteed both multiple choices and open channels of communication. Where there is free competition for people's votes (or dollars), elites must seek a more or less constant following, even while in power, in order to sustain their position and influence. Therefore, each elite must be *responsive* to its following, or risk losing it. Responsiveness of elite to non-elite is the central meaning of access, and responsiveness requires non-elite participation in choosing from among *competing* elites (or would-be elites).

However, wide participation in the selection of elites does not necessarily result in wide opportunities to be selected for inclusion in elites. Workers, for example, may not particularly care to vote for other workers who are running for office; instead of selecting people like themselves, they may prefer to support people whom they would like to be, or whom they respect. Aristocratic critics of equalitarianism argue, on the contrary, that where the community as a whole determines the membership of elites, the result will be the selection of men who share the characteristics of the greater number. According to these critics, popular participation in choosing elites lowers standards of choice because people will not prefer men who are believed to be socially superior to them. For this reason they believe that mass men will rule in the equalitarian society.

We may agree that the chances an elite will reflect in its composition and conduct the lowest common denominator of the community are higher where the community as a whole determines the membership of the elite. However, popular selection is not a sufficient condition for the rule of people who mirror the characteristics of the non-elite. If it were sufficient, then how could we explain the relatively high proportion of educated and professionally-trained people in democratically elected elites? The fact is that poorly educated people predominate in democratic electorates, yet well-educated people predominate in democratically selected governing groups. The following comparison of the educational achievement of American political leaders with that of the population at large is only one of many studies, conducted in different countries, which document this point.

TABLE 1.—Educational Level of American Political Officials.

OFFICIALS	PER CENT ATTAINING EACH LEVEL			
	None	Grade School	High School	College
Presidents, Vice-Presidents, Cabinet members (1877-1934)	0	11	10	79
Supreme Court Justices (1897-1937)	0	0	0	100
U.S. Senators (1949-1951)	0	3	10	87
U.S. Representatives (1941-1943)	0	0	12	88
Higher civil servants (1940)	0	0	7	93
State Governors (1930-1940)	0	3	20	77
Missouri State Legislators (1901-1931)	0	30	13	57
Population over 25 years (1940)	5	54	31	10

SOURCE: Matthews (1954, p. 29).

The tendency for people to choose those who are better educated exists in private as well as public groups. Thus trade unions and working-class parties tend to be led by the better-educated workers or even by middle-class intellectuals and professionals. The educational attainment of leaders of American trade unions illustrates this.

TABLE 2.—Educational Level of American Labor Officials.

OFFICIALS	PER CENT ATTAINING EACH LEVEL				
	None	Grade School	Some High School	High School Graduate	College
A.F.L. officials	1	34	26	14	25
C.I.O. officials	0	20	24	23	33
U. S. adult population	4	57	15	14	10

SOURCE: Mills (1948, p. 72).

It is not the mere fact of popular selection of elites which places mass men in elites and incites elites to accept mass standards as guides to their own conduct. It is possible for large numbers of people to recognize and accept special qualifications for membership in elites, *so long as they believe that those with special talent may gain access to institutions of higher education and training; and so long as they believe that they as non-elite also have important (if different) social functions to perform.* In short, open elites do not necessarily lead non-elites to seek to create elites in their own image, or, more generally, to engage in mass actions.

However, when elites are relatively open and unprotected, mass movements are more likely than when elites are exclusive. A comparison of France and Germany in the Late Middle Ages shows this. Outbreaks of chiliastic mass movements appear to have been most numerous in some areas of what are now northern France and Belgium from the end of the eleventh to the middle of the fourteenth century. After this time, and up to the Reformation, the main center of these movements shifted to Germany (Cohn, 1957, p. 21). Now during the period in which revolutionary chiliasm flourished in France, central authority was relatively weak and unprotected; whereas during the subsequent period, when the French monarchy established its hegemony, messianic mass movements declined. For in "a monarchy centralized to the point of despotism, controlled by a royal army and civil service . . . there was little opening for popular movements of any kind." In Germany, on the other hand, where the nation was fragmenting into a host of small states and principalities, the decline of royal power was accompanied by an upsurge of messianic movements during a period which also witnessed an increase in economic activity and population (Cohn, 1957, pp. 97-8).

Inaccessible elites prevent a high rate of mass behavior and mass movements even where, as in the Soviet Union, for example, the population is highly atomized. Repression of spontaneous behavior in all spheres of Soviet life prevents the formation of mass movements, despite the fact that all legitimate independent group life has been destroyed. In the United States, on the other hand, whatever dispositions exist to engage in mass movements may readily gain expression. Relatively easy access to the means of communication and organization (especially freedom of association and speech) accounts for the higher rate of mass movements in this country, rather than the level of atomization of the population (which is much higher in the Soviet Union).

If mass tendencies require accessible elites, so do pluralist tendencies. For without widespread opportunity to influence elites there would not be the requisite freedom to evolve and sustain the diversity of patterns of life that characterizes pluralist society. Low access, on the other hand, is a requirement of communal society, for without it the elite would be hard-pressed to maintain traditional authority. Low access also is a requirement of totalitarian society, since without it the elite could not maintain total power.

In mass society, unlike totalitarian society, power is not monopolized by a single elite. Instead, power rests in the populace as well as in the various elites. The *extent* to which the populace controls elites distinguishes mass society from totalitarian society. The *manner* in which the populace intervenes in elites distinguishes mass society from pluralist society. The populace tends to intervene directly and in an unrestrained manner in the mass society, but in the pluralist society the manner of participation is less direct and unrestrained, since the population is not available for activistic modes of behavior. In short, the level of access to elites determines *who* shall be able to participate in decision-making processes, and the level of atomization of non-elites determines *how* they shall participate. For example, when there are available elements in a society, non-elite intervention in elites may take the form of *ad hoc* pressures on decision-makers:

A major recent development in civil politics generally has been the increase in the number of points at which an administration is available to public demands. This tendency, which results in what has been labeled "mass society," is evident in such movements as "mc carthyism" in national politics, and in local movements such as that which ousted Goslin [as superintendent of the Pasadena school system]. These movements operate by mobilizing a previously apathetic mass and demanding responsiveness from an administration at those points in the decision-making process which have heretofore been shut off from public pressure. (Coleman, 1957, pp. 15-16)

Modes of access, on the other hand, may be largely *institutionalized,* so that decision-making is open to outside intervention only in prescribed ways and at prescribed times. This protects the structure of authority, while at the same time allowing for democratic participation and control. If the administration (or other types of elites) were "to be responsive to the public at *all* stages of decision-making [it] would be completely debilitating to any authority structure" (Coleman, 1957, p. 15).

Direct access to elites creates a type of elite that lacks

adequate inner resources as well as sufficient protection from external pressures to act with decisiveness and independence. People in a mass (that is, available non-elites) are inclined to adopt populist values, including diffuse anti-elitist and strongly egalitarian sentiments. Members of elites are recruited from the mass and continue to be exposed to the values of the mass, so that even they tend to accept populist values. This can only lead to a lack of security and confidence in their role as leaders. In a society where the role of leadership is not respected, the leaders themselves can hardly be expected to respect that role or their special qualifications to fill it. They do not develop the will to lead, nor a firm sense of responsibility for leadership.

Members of elites in mass society do not *feel* elite; they feel mass. As a result, elites lack the capability for strong leadership: they cannot take advantage of opportunities to strengthen a democratic order which are provided by those liberal-pluralist tendencies that may exist alongside of mass tendencies; nor can they exploit opportunities to build a totalitarian order that are provided by the presence of atomized masses. People who are capable of forming and leading a totalitarian movement emerge directly from the same population that supplies the mass following for such a movement; Hitler and Mussolini are good examples. The character of an available population now shall be examined.

Available Non-elites

People are available for mass behavior when they lack attachments to proximate objects. When people are divorced from their community and work, they are free to reunite in new ways. Furthermore, those who do not possess a variety of relations with their fellows are disposed to seek new and often remote sources of attachment and allegiance. Where proximate concerns are meaningful, people do not spend much time or energy seeking direct gratification from remote symbols. They may try to understand and influence the course of distant events, but they do so by means of and in relation to their face-to-face relations, at home, in the neighborhood, at work, in their club or union, and so forth. But when these proximate relations fail to serve major interests or to provide personal gratifications, people are likely to turn away from their local world to the "great society" in their search for new ways to satisfy their needs. This disposition will be accentuated in times of crisis, when the satisfaction of interests becomes especially difficult. In the absence of proximate sources of gratification and restraint, individuals may become highly responsive to the appeal of mass movements bent on the transformation of the world.

On the other hand, people may respond to their lack of proximate relations with apathy; as a result, their availability for mobilization may be hidden. Apathy born of alienation from community may persist under more or less stable conditions. However, the underlying disaffection of which apathy may be an expression readily leads to activism in times of crisis, as when people who have previously rejected politics turn out in large numbers to support demagogic attacks on the existing political system. Because apathetic people may not manifest their discontent directly, we must measure their availability in terms of their lack of proximate attachments. At the same time, the concept of availability entails the prediction that people who lack proximate relations are more likely to engage in mass behavior than are people who possess such relations. This pattern may characterize elites as well as non-elites, since members of elites also may lack proximate attachments. Elites, too, may look for guidance and meaning in remote places, which, from their vantage point, are the values and moods of the masses. Intellectuals may be especially ready for active service in mass movements, since they more keenly experience the lack of larger purpose than do those less given to abstract and symbolic activities.[19]

Our diagram of four types of society indicates that an available population is a requirement for totalitarianism as well as for mass society. But mass movements are not characteristic of totalitarian society. All forms of spontaneous collective activity, especially those directed at social change, are suppressed by the totalitarian regime. Collective activity in the Soviet Union, for example, tends to be tightly controlled from above in all spheres of life. A totalitarian regime requires atomized masses in order to be able to use them to acquire power, and subsequently in order to keep them from forming alternative loyalties independent of the regime. Totalitarian society, from this standpoint, is the totally mobilized society: it is one gigantic movement controlled by the elite. It is only insofar as the population is kept in motion that the society can be a thorough-going totalitarianism. Once large numbers are able to express their dispositions, they tend to withdraw from active participation in society; or they will act apart from the regime. Spontaneous behavior in whatever guise and area threatens the totalitarianism of society.

Thus, totalitarian control depends on institutionalizing high availability. This follows from the requirement of total domination: all aspects of people's lives must be organized and controlled. The mere fact of an available population is a strong pressure on an elite with dictatorial ambitions to institute such control-in-depth, since the behavior of people who are unattached is highly unpredictable and potentially explosive. The non-elite also needs to form and maintain hyper-attachments to the elite in totalitarian society, for since people are given no other choice as to objects of attachment, they must find psychological sustenance in this manner or do without it. The "confessions" of the Moscow Trials may have been in part manifestations of this over-commit-

_____
19. The situation of intellectuals is explored in detail in Chapter 10 below.

ment to extreme collectivism, and the absence of all other significant attachments:[20] the Communist movement was the only "world" that had any meaning for the old Bolsheviks.[21] An alternative is withdrawal from all attachments in the face of "futures pitilessly blocked and passions violently choked by oppressive discipline . . . [of an] excessive physical or moral despotism" (Durkheim, 1951, p. 276).

The difference between mass society and totalitarian society with respect to the condition of the population may be summarized as follows. In both instances people are available, but in mass society they are free to engage in various kinds of efforts to overcome the tensions inherent in this condition, including either withdrawal from the public arena or activism in it; whereas in totalitarian society they are forced into activism in the service of the elite. People have to participate in the totalitarian movement in totalitarian society, but they may choose to do so in the mass society. If enough people make this choice in mass society, the totalitarian movement may become sufficiently strong to transform mass society into totalitarian society—in which case participation no longer is a matter of choice. Thus, the totalitarian movement is the link between mass society and totalitarian society.

A population which is integrated into a set of proximate relations is a requirement for our other two types of society. Communal society requires an unavailable population in order to maintain its strong traditionalism, since large numbers of unattached people would constitute a continuous source of new (non-traditional) forms of integration. Pluralist society requires an unavailable population in order to maintain its freedom and diversity.

The pluralistic society keeps men's sentiments from flying outwards towards fixation on those remote objects which unsettle equanimity and disturb the pluralistic equilibrium. A well-work-

---

20. Cf. Durkheim's discussion of "altruistic suicide" (1951, pp. 220-1).

21. On this interpretation of the Moscow trials, see especially Koestler (1941).

ing pluralistic society absorbs sufficient of the attention and affection of its members into a wide range of more proximate concerns—workshop, neighborhood, club, church, team, family, friends, trade union, school, etc. At least as important, it keeps down the need for a unification of all these loyalties into a single loyalty. It confines the tendency, aroused and aggravated by crises, to fuse them all together into a single organism under a single standard. Not only does pluralism keep the loyalties from moving towards a single and remote object such as the nation, it limits the demand that the loyalties of others should be organized in that manner. (Shils, 1956, p. 159)

Unlike pluralist society, mass society does not keep men's sentiments from fastening on remote objects, precisely because it fails to absorb enough of the interest and emotions of its members into a variety of proximate concerns. This means concretely that (1) a greater proportion of people with few proximate concerns as compared to people with many such attachments, tend to be apathetic and uninformed on public matters; but that (2) in times of crisis a greater proportion of people with few proximate concerns discard apathy and engage in mass movements outside of and against the institutional order. There is evidence from a wide variety of empirical studies that these two modes of response are characteristic of the socially atomized segments of society.

TABLE 3.—Interest in Political Affairs by Group Members and Non-Members.

PER CENT WHO:	Group Members	Non-Members
Expressed opinions on China policy	91	85
Expressed opinions on atomic energy policy	78	59
Discussed atomic bomb in last week	43	24
Discussed relations with Russia in last week	53	31
Say they voted in last presidential election	72	63

SOURCE: Hyman and Sheatsley (1954, p. 62).

That lack of proximate relations is associated with the lack of day-to-day concern for national and international affairs is indicated by a national survey (1947) which shows that members of voluntary organizations are more likely to hold opinions about issues, are more likely to discuss these opinions, and are more likely to seek their implementation than are those who belong to no organizations (Table 3).

It is particularly with respect to national and international affairs that we would expect people to be indifferent or only superficially interested unless they were involved in some sort of group activity *through which distant events are linked to proximate meanings.*[22] People who do not participate in organized activity are less likely to understand distant events, so that a major crisis which suddenly thrusts such events into personal situations finds previous non-participants readily available for highly irrational and extremist interpretations of them.

Several studies show that non-voters constitute a "more or less socially isolated segment of the population. Non-voting is merely one manifestation of the weak linkage of a category of the population to social affairs generally" (Key, 1952, p. 580). A 1952 election study of Pittsfield, Massachusetts, found that non-voters were less likely to (1) belong to voluntary associations (52% of the non-voters held no memberships, versus 29% of the voters), (2) expose themselves to political communication, (3) acquire political information, (4) identify with a political group, (5) express an opinion on current political issues (Hastings, 1954). It was further found that "with age, income, education, sex, and religion held constant, as voting decreased, so did social

---

22. One study reports that individuals varied in the degree to which their attitudes toward Russia were related to more general values. Individuals for whom Russia did not "engage" their general values lacked interests and activities broad enough to include that object. "Since foreign affairs are rather distant from the immediate concerns of daily life, some breadth of interests is required for a person to extend his values to so remote an area" (M. Brewster Smith, "Personal Values as Determinants of a Political Attitude," cited in Hyman and Sheatsley [1954, p. 63]). Of course, certain types of groups are more capable of increasing the breadth of their members' interests than are others. An organization devoted to the discussion of public questions obviously is going to have a much greater impact in this respect than is an athletic club.

involvement in general" (Hastings, 1956, p. 304). Finally, that "nonreliance on the electoral process by substantial social groups increases their availability to the appeals of the demagogue" (Janowitz and Marvick, 1956, p. 98), is indicated by the greater willingness of Pittsfield non-voters than voters to express support for McCarthy (see Table 4).

TABLE 4.—Support for McCarthy by Voters and Non-Voters.

Support for McCarthy*	Voters	Non-Voters
Yes	13%	20%
No	79	36
Depends or DK	8	44
N	(112)	(44)

* The exact question was "Would you like to have McCarthy on your party ticket as the candidate for senator from Massachusetts?"

SOURCE: Hastings (1956, p. 305).

The difference between voters and non-voters in willingness to reject McCarthy was not due to differences in age, sex, income, education, or religion. All of the evidence in the Pittsfield study suggests that it is the non-voter's *social isolation* which makes him apathetic and poorly committed to established institutions.

A recent analysis of community conflict in the United States shows that poorly integrated sections of the community are most likely to engage in mass action outside and often against established social institutions in times of crisis. For people with few social and psychological ties to the community are subject to less social or self control. Such people tend to be concentrated in the lower social strata of the community. As a consequence of their greater social isolation,

(a) lower-status people will less often be drawn into community controversy; (b) when they are drawn into controversy, they will be less constrained in their activities and quicker to reduce the controversy to personal derogation and attack. *Note that these two consequences arise not from anything intrinsically "different" about lower-status people, but only from their differential participation in community activities.* In recent school controversies, for instance, these consequences are similarly evident among high-status persons who were previously inactive in community organizations. (Coleman, 1957, pp. 21-2; italics added)

If it is true that those who are socially isolated feel less bound to employ legitimate methods in community controversies, then we would expect to find a close association between community involvement and support for civil liberties in the United States (where civil liberties are institutional norms). Support for civil liberties may be interpreted as a belief in the importance of using legitimate methods, rather than direct action against opponents, in carrying on social conflict. Community leaders may be considered to be more closely tied to the social order than are non-leaders. Therefore, community leaders should be found to express greater support for civil liberties than a cross-section of the community. A recent study shows that community leaders tend to be much more willing to express their support for free speech and association for nonconformists (e.g., socialists and Communists) than is the community as a whole. Specifically, whereas 66% of the average of community leaders in several cities are "relatively more tolerant" toward nonconformists, only 32% of the cross-section of the same cities expressed themselves in this manner (Stouffer, 1955, p. 52). This difference between leaders and the community at large does not seem to be due simply to education, since 79% of the college educated leaders are among the more tolerant as compared with 66% for the general college educated population (pp. 90, 104). Furthermore, *all* kinds of community leaders scored higher than the community average: more than 75% of newspaper publishers, chairmen of community chests, presidents of library boards, and presidents of bar associations were relatively tolerant; between 60% and 70% of presidents of P.T.A.s and school boards, chairmen of Republican and Democratic county central committees, presidents of chambers of commerce and labor unions, and mayors were also relatively tolerant; and so were between 45% and 50% of the presidents of women's clubs, regents of the D.A.R., and commanders of the American Legion (p. 52).

If leaders of community groups possess firmer relations to the social order than do non-leaders and therefore are more willing to abide by libertarian norms, higher status people generally are more likely to participate in public life and also to support civil liberties. Table 5 summarizes many studies on the support for civil liberties by different educational and occupational strata. Table 6 summarizes many studies on participation in the community by different socioeconomic strata. Participation is measured by membership, activity, and leadership in voluntary associations; and by feelings of ability and obligation to participate in the political process.

Taken together these tables show that low status people are less involved in the community and are less libertarian in their beliefs. The tables do not show that low status people are less libertarian *because* they are less involved in the community. One bit of evidence in support of the contention that non-participation tends to lessen commitment to democratic values is contained in a study of a sample drawn from the West German electorate in 1953. Table 7 shows that among manual workers and, to a lesser extent, among white-collar workers, those who belong to at least one voluntary association are more likely to favor a democratic party system than are non-members.

TABLE 5.—Libertarian-Authoritarian Attitudes Among Different Educational and Occupational Strata.

PER CENT WHO:		EDUCATION			OCCUPATION		
		College	High School	Grade School	Professional and Business	White-Collar	Manual
Favor prohibiting Communist party membership by law[a]	1947	46		66	56	57	66
	1949	54		71			
Oppose right of newspaper to criticize government[b]	1945	14	27	41			
	1948	9	21	43			
Oppose right of Communists to use the radio[c]	1945	29	43	42			
	1948	48	57	62			
Oppose releasing conscientious objectors[d]	1946	18	23	25			
Score among "less tolerant" on civil liberties scale[e]	1954	7	14	22			
Score high on "authoritarianism" (F scale)[f]	1948	20	28		21		28
	1953	33	59	81	30	59	64
Oppose European immigration to U.S.[g]	1945	41	52	52			
Believe average Japanese disloyal to U.S.[h]	1946	13	23	31			
Oppose job equality for Negroes[i]	1948	13	15	27			
Think Negroes treated fairly[j]	1946	51	67	70	57	59	72
Believe need for Congressional investigation of communism in churches[k]	1953	20		45			
Oppose discussion of communism in college classes[l]	1949	12		28			
	1954	16		31			
Oppose allowing ex-Communists to teach in college[m]	1953	50		69			
Are anti-Semitic (Germany)[n]	1946	48	54	63			
Oppose colored immigration (Australia)[o]	1943				43	54	59

SOURCES: a. Hyman and Sheatsley (1953, p. 8), reporting data from Gallup polls. b. "Opinion News," Sept. 15, 1948, p. 11. c. Ibid. d. Cantril (1951, p. 135). e. Data recomputed from Stouffer (1955, p. 90). f. Janowitz and Marvick (1953, p. 192); MacKinnon and Centers (1956, pp. 615-17). g. Cantril (1951, p. 307). h. "Opinion News," March 1, 1948. i. "Public Opinion Quarterly" (1949, p. 166). j. "Opinion News," February 15, 1948, p. 5. k. Hyman and Sheatsley (1953, p. 9). l. Ibid., p. 12. m. Ibid. n. "Opinion News," March 1, 1948, p. 7. o. Cantril (1951, p. 306).

TABLE 6.—Social Participation as Related to Socioeconomic Status.

SOCIAL PARTICIPATION   SOCIOECONOMIC LEVEL

Per cent who have memberships in voluntary associations:	Business class	Working class
One or more memberships	95	46
Two or more memberships	81	18

SOURCE: (Muncie, 1924)a

	Social Class					
Per cent who:	Upper-upper	Lower-upper	Upper-middle	Lower-middle	Upper-lower	Lower-lower
Have one or more memberships in voluntary associations	72	71	64	49	39	22
Ratio of political posts held by a class to its proportion of the total population (approximations)	2	2	2	1	1	¼

SOURCE: (Yankee City, 1935)b

	Occupation				
Per cent who have memberships in voluntary associations:	Professional	Business	White Collar	Skilled	Unskilled
One or more memberships	79	67	47	44	32
Two or more memberships	62	37	17	11	7

SOURCE: (New York, 1935)c

	Socioeconomic Status Level			
Per cent who:	A,B	C+	C—	D
Have one or more memberships in voluntary associations	72	56	44	35

SOURCE: (Erie County, 1940)d

Per cent who are members or leaders of voluntary associations:	Income	
	$1200 or more (top ⅓)	Less than $1200
Have one or more memberships	96	80
Have two or more memberships	73	34
Hold leadership positions	(Those earning $1200 or more four times as likely as those earning less than $1200.)	

SOURCE: (Franklin, 1940)e

Per cent who have memberships in voluntary associations:	Prestige Class		
	High	Medium	Low
One or more memberships	96	64	36
Three or more memberships	69	20	2

SOURCE: (New York rural community, 1940)f

TABLE 6 (Continued)

SOCIAL PARTICIPATION	SOCIOECONOMIC LEVEL		
	Economic Status		
Per cent of farmers who:	High	Medium	Low
Belong to a farm organization	50	29	13

SOURCE: (United States, 1943)g

	Income		
Per cent who:	$7000 & over	$3000-6999	Under $3000
Have one or more formal memberships in associations	81	65	42
Are very active in organization(s)	21	12	8
Frequently associate with co-workers	28	22	12
Frequently associate with neighbors	44	37	37

SOURCE: (Detroit, 1953)h

	Income					
Per cent who have memberships in:	$7500 & over	$5000-7499	$4000-4999	$3000-3999	$2000-2999	Under $2000
No organization	48	57	65	71	71	76
One organization	22	22	21	18	17	17
Two or more organizations	30	21	14	11	12	7

SOURCE: (United States, 1955)i

	Socioeconomic Status	
	High	Low
Chapin's Participation Scale score (men)	21.81	0.55
Radius of travel during lifetime	1100 miles	145 miles
Per cent who frequently visit friends outside neighborhood	91	27

SOURCE: (Prairieton, South Dakota, 1942)j

	Income		
	$6000 and over	$3000-5999	Under $3000
Community participation score	4.24	2.84	2.17

SOURCE: (Small Oregon town, 1954)k

	Economic Level			
Per cent whose political participation is:	A	B	C	D
Very high	36	24	11	3
Fairly high	33	26	19	9
Fairly low	23	34	38	31
Very low	8	16	32	57

SOURCE: (United States, 1950)l

	Income				
Per cent who:	$5000 & over	$4000-4999	$3000-3999	$2000-2999	Under $2000
Voted in 1948	82	75	74	61	46
Voted in 1952	88	83	76	68	53

SOURCE: (United States, 1948 and 1952)m

TABLE 6 (Continued)

SOCIAL PARTICIPATION			SOCIOECONOMIC LEVEL	
Per cent who:	$5000 & over	$4000-4999 $3000-3999 $2000-2999		Under $2000
Feel high sense of citizen duty to vote	58	43 39 41		31
Have high sense of political efficacy	43	33 25 19		11

SOURCE: (United States, 1952)n
a. Lynd and Lynd (1929, p. 528). b. Warner and Lunt (1941, pp. 329-34). c. Komarovsky (1949, p. 381). d. Lazarsfeld et al. (1948, p. 173). e. Mather (1941, p. 381). f. Regrouping of data from Kaufman (1953, p. 199). g. Cantril (1951, p. 5). h. Axelrod (1956, pp. 15-17). i. Wright and Hyman (1958, p. 289). j. Useem et al. (1949, pp. 457, 459). k. Foskett (1955, pp. 431-8). l. Woodward and Roper (1950, p. 877). m. Campbell et al. (1954, p. 73). n. Ibid., p. 197 and p. 191.

TABLE 7.—Party System Preferred by Occupation and Membership in Voluntary Associations, Germany, 1953 (Men Only).

PARTY SYSTEM PREFERRED	MANUAL		WHITE-COLLAR	
	Members	Non-members	Members	Non-members
Multi-party system	68%	45%	86%	77%
One or no party	24	43	11	21
No opinion	7	12	3	2
N	(145)	(121)	(182)	(48)

SOURCE: Linz (1958).

A national sample of American workers also shows a relationship between membership and participation in voluntary associations, on the one hand, and non-authoritarian attitudes, on the other (see Table 8).[23]

TABLE 8.—Authoritarian Attitudes by Membership in Voluntary Associations, Manual Workers Only.

AUTHORITARIAN ATTITUDES	NUMBER OF MEMBERSHIPS			NUMBER OF ACTIVE MEMBERSHIPS		
	0	1	2+	0	1	2+
High	39%	29%	27%	35%	34%	17%
Medium	39	47	31	42	26	48
Low	22	24	42	24	40	34
N	(92)	(87)	(64)	(165)	(47)	(29)

SOURCE: Computed from national survey data supplied by the Survey Research Center, University of Michigan.

23. Robert Lane's analysis of the same data produced different results. This appears to be due to different measures of authoritarianism (Lane used only four items in the form of a Guttman-type scale, whereas we used all ten items in the survey), and different measures of group membership (Lane divided the cases between those with 0-2 memberships and those with 3 or more memberships, whereas we used three breaks). See Lane (1955, pp. 173-79).

Non-participation results in lack of exposure to information and indoctrination concerning democratic values, and in the lack of habits of discussion, debate, negotiation, and compromise—modes of conduct indispensable to democratic politics. This factor of non-participation may be added to other aspects of low status which are not favorable to libertarianism, such as insecurity resulting from poorly-paid and uncertain jobs, and lack of sophistication and understanding of civil liberties resulting from poor education. People who occupy a low status are especially susceptible to the belief that all personal misfortunes are due to conspiracies against them, and that the world is divided into "people who run things" and "people like us." They are readily attracted to ideologies which paint moral issues in rigid and absolutistic terms. This is indicated by the negative association between status and sectarianism: the lower occupational and educational strata manifest the higher preference for ethnocentrism, evangelism, and emotionalism in religion. Conversely, the higher social strata prefer the institutional and liturgical church which accepts the social order and integrates existing cultural definitions into its religious life (Dynes, 1955).

But *in times of crisis mass movements and totalitarian parties acquire support from all social strata,* as we shall show in detail in Part III. It will be seen that within all strata, people divorced from community, occupation, and association are first and foremost among the supporters of extremism. The decisive social process in mass society is the *atomization* of social relations; even though this process is accentuated in the lower strata, it operates throughout the society.

Chapter 3

Structure
of Mass Society

WE CAN conceive of all but the simplest societies as comprising three levels of social relations. The first level consists of highly personal or primary relations, notably the family. The third level contains relations inclusive of the whole population, notably the state. The second level comprises all intermediate relations, notably the local community, voluntary association, and occupational group. These intermediate relations function as links between the individual and his primary relations, on the one hand, and the state and other national relations, on the other hand. It must be emphasized that voluntary associations are not the only kind of intermediate relation; all organized relations that mediate between the family and the nation, such as local government and the local press, are classified as intermediate structures in the present study. Voluntary associations are used as the main empirical indicators of intermediate structures in this study because the best data are available for this kind of intermediate relation.

The logic of our model dictates that the structure of mass society must be of such a nature as to support a high rate of mass behavior by fulfilling the two requirements for mass behavior, namely, accessible elites and available non-elites. Such a structure may be shown to be one in which intermediate relations of community, occupation, and association are more or less inoperative, and therefore one in which the individual and primary group are directly related to the state and to nation-wide organizations. The members of mass society, then, are interconnected only by virtue of their common ties to national centers of communication and organization. It is in this sense that we speak of mass society as the *atomized* society.

Mass society lacks intermediate relations, but it is not to be conceived merely as the absence of social relations. The central feature of primary groups in mass society is not so much their internal weakness as it is their external *isolation* from the larger society. The isolation of primary groups means that by themselves they cannot provide the basis for participation in the larger society. Again, mass society is not to be thought of as lacking relations inclusive of the whole population. On the contrary, modern mass society possesses a highly *politicized* organization, as "everything that people know or feel Society will not undertake is simply heaped on to the . . . State" (Burckhardt, 1955, p. 203). This results in the centralization of the social structure, especially a centralized state. The centralization of communication and decision-making means that to the extent people do participate in the larger society, they must do so through the state, and other inclusive (nation-wide) structures.[24]

We shall elaborate this model of the structure of mass society by examining it on each of its three levels: (1) the weakness of intermediate relations, (2) the isolation of primary relations, and (3) the centralization of national relations.

---

24. Centralization, it must be emphasized, does not necessarily mean authoritarianism. Thus Lasswell and Kaplan (1950, pp. 224-5, 235) distinguish between "centralization" and "concentration" of power, and include the latter but exclude the former on a list of seven definitive characteristics of despotic as against democratic rule.

Weakness of Intermediate Relations

Weak intermediate relations leave elites and non-elites directly exposed to one another, and thereby invite widespread mass behavior; for in the absence of intermediate relations, participation in the larger society must be direct rather than filtered through intervening relationships.

The lack of strong independent groups undermines multiple proximate concerns, and thereby increases mass availability. Consider a man's relation to his work. While there often are important sources of intrinsic satisfaction derivable from the work itself, nevertheless the gratification derived from a sense of fellowship and control over the conditions of work are at least as important for firm occupational attachments. It is precisely these latter sources of interest and participation in work that require independent groups for their realization. Informal work groups supply some basis for fellowship and control at work, but with the growth in scale and complexity of the factory, office, and work institutions generally, they are insufficient. Therefore, all kinds of formal work associations, such as trade unions and professional associations, are needed.[25] To the extent that they fail to develop, or, at the other extreme, themselves grow so far out of the reach of their members as to no longer be capable of providing the individual with a sense of participation and control, people are less likely to find the whole sphere of work an interesting and rewarding experience. Consequently, people may cease to care about their work, though of course they continue to work, despite their alienation from their jobs.

Similar factors shape a man's relation to his community. Unless a variety of forms of association are open to him, the

---

25. Durkheim judged occupational groups to be the basic kind of intermediate organization in modern society (1958, pp. 1-41, 96-97).

individual is not likely to take an active interest in civic affairs—particularly in the metropolis, where the size of the population and the specialization of activities place a premium on voluntary associations as bases of political participation. Or, in the absence of associations such as the P.T.A. to provide channels of communication and influence between parents and school, the individual is less likely to develop or sustain interest and participation in the education of his children. Examples may be easily multiplied, but these are sufficient to suggest why independent groups are indispensable bases for the maintenance of meaningful proximate concerns.

The lack of a structure of independent groups also removes the basis for self-protection on the part of elites, because it permits direct modes of intervention to replace mediated participation in elites. In the first place, intermediate groups, even though they are independent of top elites, operate to protect these elites from arbitrary and excessive pressures by themselves being responsive to the needs and demands of people. They carry a large share of the burden of seeking to fulfill the interests of people who would otherwise have to rely exclusively on national agencies to minister to their needs. Secondly, the leaders of intermediate groups, irrespective of their particular aims (so long as these aims are not contrary to the integrity of the community), help to shore up the larger system of authority with which their own authority is inextricably bound. Third, intermediate groups help to protect elites by functioning as channels through which popular participation in the larger society (especially in the national elites) may be directed and restrained. In the absence of intermediate groups to act as representatives and guides for popular participation, people must act *directly* in the critical centers of society, and therefore in a manner unrestrained by the values and interests of a variety of social groups.

These reasons why the weakness of intermediate groups

characterize mass society are at the same time reasons why the strength of such groups characterizes the pluralist society. A strong intermediate structure consists of stable and independent groups which represent diverse and frequently conflicting interests. The opposition among such groups restrains one another's power, thereby limiting the aggregate intervention in elites; that is, a system of social checks and balances among a plurality of diverse groups operates to protect elites as well as non-elites in ways we have indicated. Furthermore, the separation of the various spheres of society—for example, separation of religion and politics —means that access to elites in one sphere does not directly affect elites in other spheres. The various authorities are more or less autonomous in their own spheres, in that they are not directly determined in their membership or policy by authorities in other spheres. These same factors protect non-elites from elites, since independent groups guard their members from one another, and since overlapping memberships among groups, *each of which concerns only limited aspects of its members' lives,* restrains each group from seeking total domination over its membership.

The state in pluralist society also plays a vital role in support of individual freedom, for it is above all the state which has the capacity to safeguard the individual against domination by particular groups. Durkheim saw more profoundly than most that it is the *combination* of the state and what he called "secondary groups" that engenders individual liberty, rather than one or the other social structure alone. We shall quote him at length because he brings out with great clarity the special competence of each type of social structure for the advancement of individual freedom:

[The individual] must not be curbed and monopolised by the secondary groups, and these groups must not be able to get a mastery over their members and mould them at will. There must therefore exist above these local, domestic—in a word, secondary —authorities, some overall authority which makes the law for them all: it must remind each of them that it is but a part and not the whole and that it should not keep for itself what rightly belongs to the whole. The only means of averting this collective particularism and all it involves for the individual, is to have a special agency with the duty of representing the overall collectivity, its rights and its interests, vis-à-vis these individual collectivities. . . . It is solely because, in holding its constituent societies in check, it [the state] prevents them from exerting the repressive influences over the individual that they would otherwise exert. So there is nothing inherently tyrannical about State intervention in the different fields of collective life; on the contrary, it has the object and the effect of alleviating tyrannies that do exist. It will be argued, might not the State in turn become despotic? Undoubtedly, provided there was nothing to counter that trend. In that case, as the sole existing collective force, it produces the effects that any collective force not neutralized by any counter-force of the same kind would have on individuals. The State itself then becomes a leveller and repressive. And its repressiveness becomes even harder to endure than that of small groups, because it is more artificial. The State, in our large-scale societies, is so removed from individual interests that it cannot take into account the special or local and other conditions in which they exist. Therefore when it does attempt to regulate them, it succeeds only at the cost of doing violence to them and distorting them. It is, too, not sufficiently in touch with individuals in the mass to be able to mould them inwardly, so that they readily accept its pressure on them. The individual eludes the State to some extent—the State can only be effective in the context of a large-scale society—and individual diversity may not come to light. Hence, all kinds of resistance and distressing conflicts arise. The small groups do not have this drawback. They are close enough to the things that provide their *raison d'être* to be able to adapt their actions exactly and they surround the individuals closely enough to shape them in their own image. The inference to be drawn from this comment, however, is simply that *if that collective force, the State, is to be the liberator of the individual, it has itself need of some counterbalance; it must be restrained by other collective forces, that is, by . . . secondary groups . . . it is out of this conflict of social forces that individual liberties are born.* (Durkheim, 1958, pp. 62-3; italics added)

It has been said that medieval society was in fact essentially pluralist.[26] But of course medieval society did not permit democratic control. The confusion here resides in the notion of pluralism: shall it be conceived as referring merely to a multiplicity of associations, or in addition, to a multiplicity of *affiliations?* Where individuals belong to several groups, no one group is *inclusive* of its members' lives. Associations have members with a variety of social characteristics (e.g., class and ethnic identities) and group memberships (e.g., trade unions may possess members who go to various churches, or even belong to church-affiliated trade union associations such as ACTU). Warner found that in Newburyport, Massachusetts, one-third of the 357 associations that were studied had members from three out of the six classes he identified, another third had members from four classes, and one-sixth from five or six classes. Almost two-thirds of the 12,876 members of associations belonged to associations in which four or more of the six classes were represented. Over three-fourths belonged to associations in which three or more of the ten ethnic groups were represented. Over one-half belonged to associations in which two or more of the four religious faiths were represented (Warner and Lunt, 1941, pp. 341, 346, 349). Such extensive *cross-cutting solidarities* favor a high level of freedom and consensus: these solidarities help prevent one line of social cleavage from becoming dominant, and they constrain associations to respect the various affiliations of their members lest they alienate them. Socially heterogeneous religious organizations are also important pluralistic agencies; they may be contrasted with situations in which religious and class lines tend to closely correspond, as in France where anti-clericalism is largely a working-class phenomenon. Political parties which draw their support from all major social segments constitute still another kind of cross-cutting solidarity. In this respect, the highly heterogeneous and decentralized American parties may be con-

---

26. See, for example, Kerr (1955, p. 4).

trasted with the highly centralized, class-based Socialist parties and religious-based Catholic parties characteristic of European multiparty systems.

Our conception of pluralism includes that of multiple affiliations, which means that medieval society was not pluralist in our use of the term. So long as no association claims or receives hegemony over many aspects of its memmers' lives, its power over the individual will be limited. This is a vital point, because the authority of a private group can be as oppressive as that of the state.

A plurality of groups that are both independent and non-inclusive not only protects elites and non-elites from one another but does so in a manner that permits liberal democratic control. Liberal democratic control requires that people have *access* to elites, and that they exercise *restraint* in their participation. Independent groups help to maintain access to top-level decision-making by bringing organized pressure to bear on elites to remain responsive to outside influence. Each group has interests of its own in gaining access to elites, and has organized power not available to separate individuals for the implementation of these interests. These interests require not only that elites pay attention to the demands of the group, but also that other groups do not become so strong as to be able to shut off this group's access to the elite. Since independent groups seek to maintain their position by checking one another's power as well as the power of higher-level elites, the interaction of these groups helps to sustain access to decision-making processes in the larger society.

A plurality of independent groups also helps to regulate popular participation by integrating people into a wide range of proximate concerns. Where people possess multiple interests and commitments, attachments to remote objects, such as loyalty to the nation-state, are mediated by proximate relations.[27] Therefore, people in pluralist society engage in relatively little *direct* participation in national decisions, not because elites prevent them from doing so, but because they can influence decisions more effectively through their own groups. Furthermore, people tend to be *selective* in their participation, limiting their direct involvement in the larger society to matters that appear to them of particular concern in light of their values and interests. Since pluralist society engenders a variety of values and interests, self-selective involvement in national politics tends to limit the number of people who are vitally concerned with any given issue.

The intermediate structure of pluralist society helps to maintain access to elites by virtue of its *independence* from elites. The intermediate structure of totalitarian society, on the other hand, helps to prevent access to the elite by virtue of its *domination* by the elite. By means of intermediate groups instituted and controlled from above, the totalitarian regime is able to keep the population in a state of mobilization. Such organizations as Soviet trade unions have the primary function of activating and channelizing the energies of workers in directions determined by the regime. If there were no controlled intermediate organizations in all spheres of society, people would be free to regroup along lines independent of the regime. That is why it is of the utmost importance to totalitarian regimes to keep the population active in these controlled groups. Totalitarian regimes search out all independent forms of organizations in order to transform them or destroy them. In certain other societies, the natural decline of independent forms of associ-

---

27. See Grodzins (1956, pp. 29-30) for a discussion of the combination of direct and indirect ties to the nation-state in pluralist society: "National loyalty has a variety of roots. It springs from direct involvement in the nation's grandeur, from direct response to the symbols of the nation. It is an indirect product of satisfactory private life, loyalties to voluntary groups being transmitted to, and culminating in, national loyalty."

ation prepares the way for the rise of totalitarian movements.

The intermediate structure of communal society helps to maintain traditional authority and community in that its constituent groups are independent of the highest elites, while at the same time exercising *inclusive* control over their members—who are not free to leave the group or to join another group.[28] This kind of intermediate structure is exemplified in the corporations of the Middle Ages.

> In the Middle Ages men thought and acted corporately. The status of every man was fixed by his place in some community— manor, borough, guild, learned University or convent. The villein and the monk scarcely existed in the eye of the law except through the lord of the manor and the Abbot of the monastery. . . . The unit of medieval society was neither the nation nor the individual but something between the two—the corporation. (Trevelyan, 1953, p. 239)

The corporation protected the individual from outside coercion—for example, from undue interference by the king; but at the same time, the individual had little control over his corporate group, for he had neither status nor rights apart from the group. "As a human being, or as an English subject, no man had 'rights' either to employment or to the vote, or indeed to anything very much beyond a little Christian charity" (Trevelyan, 1953, p. 239).

The intermediate structure corresponding to each of our four types of society has been analyzed along two dimensions: (a) the strength of intermediate social organizations, especially their capacity to operate as autonomous centers of power; and (b) the inclusiveness of intermediate organizations, that is, the extent to which they encompass all aspects of their members' lives. The results of our analysis may be summarized in the form of a diagram.

---

28. Simmel has remarked that the "peculiar character of group formation in the Middle Ages" lies in the fact that "affiliation with a group absorbed the whole man" (1955, pp. 148-9).

		Strong	Weak
INTERMEDIATE GROUPS ARE:	Inclusive	communal society	totalitarian society
	Non-Inclusive	pluralist society	mass society

The table above is headed "INTERMEDIATE GROUPS ARE:" (across top, over Strong/Weak) and "INTERMEDIATE GROUPS ARE:" (down the side, over Inclusive/Non-Inclusive).

France provides a good illustration of a society in which intermediate relations are weak and non-inclusive. A closer look at this aspect of French life may help to clarify our conception of mass structure.

French society tends to be highly organized on the national level, in the form of a highly centralized state bureaucracy, and on the family level. There is a relative paucity of intermediate structures to link these two levels of life. Since voluntary associations are major forms of intermediation in the democratic society, the weakness of this social form in France, compared with England or the United States, is one important indication of the atomization of that society.

France has a long history of hostility toward voluntary associations:

French tradition has not been favourable to the growth of associations. . . . It is only within the last thirty years that the bonds of a restraining vigilance have been finally relaxed. . . . It seems clear enough that what associations, whether religious or secular, were able to exist, were the offspring of a privilege tardily given and illiberally exercised. (Laski, 1919, p. 321)

Freedom of association was not granted full legal recognition until 1901; but even since that time, a marked retardation in voluntary organization has persisted in France. Arnold Rose reports, on the basis of interviews with a number of French leaders,

the almost uniform impression that what social influence associations [those actively directed toward an outside purpose] there are in France are largely "paper" organizations and that even if they claim a large membership they do not involve the members' interests and emotions very deeply. . . . The general impression is that associations play but a small role, both in the functioning of the community or nation and in the lives of the average citizens. (1954, p. 77)

Another recent study of French society also observed "the relative scarcity of voluntary organizations in France as compared with the massive American proliferation of channels whereby individuals engage themselves in public enterprise."

The absence of active civic participation is evident in all social classes in France. There are very few "clubs" of the sort developed by the upper social groups in Britain. Among the middle class there are few parallels of Rotary, Kiwanis, and Lions . . . [or of] the Parent-Teachers' Association, the League of Women Voters, and the Association of University Women. . . . Among the working class only the labour union has made any headway, but even it hardly touches the French worker in his daily life— offering him neither educational opportunities, recreational facilities, consumers' cooperatives, nor social diversions. (Lerner, 1957, p. 29)

Voluntary groups generally tend to be shut out from participation in the performance of vital social functions in France, with the consequence that they are incapable of helping to adapt people to changing social circumstances. This appears to be true for associations nominally oriented toward change as well as for associations with conservative ideologies; French trade unions and working-class parties, for example, frequently resist change just as strenuously as do agricultural organizations and business associations. A study of associations in two French communities arrives at the conclusion that French associations are less capable of mediating social change than are their American counterparts: "The association in the United States may be a mechanism for integrating or mediating change, but in the French community, associations appear to be oriented toward the prevention of change" (Gallagher, 1957, p. 159) .

Harold Laski believed that the "division of French

parties into a plethora of groups owes its origin less to any inherent naturalness or to a proved benefit in the performance of party-functions than to the possibility such division affords for the erection of a system of loyalties external to that of the state" (Laski, 1919, p. 322). Yet, even political parties do not absorb the attention of very many Frenchmen. When asked, "Do you think it would make much difference whether one party or another were in power?" thirty-nine per cent of a national sample answered negatively and an additional 12% had no opinion. In answer to the question, "Do questions concerning politics interest you?" only 10% indicated a great interest, 39% expressed little interest, and 51% said they had no interest at all (Rose, 1954, pp. 111-13). These data suggest that French political parties are not by themselves very effective links between a large portion of the population and the national society.

Local government in France also does not function as an independent intermediate structure, since it operates more as a part of the national bureaucracy than as an expression of the autonomy of the local community. The key agent of local government, the Prefect, is appointed by the Minister of the Interior and exercises the national government's powers in a local area (department). Since these powers are great, including as they do extensive executive and financial controls, local self-government is small. Local government is a mechanism of national authority, and not a basis for local participation and control. Therefore, it does not serve to involve the individual in the public realm, nor does it serve to protect the individual against control by the state.

To an inconceivable degree Empire and Republic have completed the work of the monarchy and extinguished all trace of autonomy and independence in communes and departments. The first and most important answer to the question of who rules France must be that it is ruled by ninety agents [Prefects] of the Ministry of the Interior. (Luethy, 1957, p. 20)

The local community and parish in France may provide certain satisfactions for the individual. The cafe and public parks are bases of participation in the local community.[29] But institutions of this type, no matter how much they may enrich communal life, are nevertheless not capable of link- ing either the individual or the community to the larger society. Furthermore, increasing geographic mobility is weakening these informal social relations. As for the parish, a recent inquiry notes that "the larger part of even rural France consists of 'parishes indifferent to Christian tradi- tions' " and concludes that "the church does not have much hold over a majority of the French today" (Rose, 1954, pp. 106-7). The apparent ineffectiveness of local government, community, and parish as bases of participation in the larger society creates a social vacuum in French life. This may be a reason why a study of a French community, after reporting that associations are "generally not very impor- tant" and "cut into the lives of their members very little," nevertheless concludes that "without the associations, [people] would live in almost complete isolation."[30]

We may conclude from this brief analysis of French group life that independent social forms are more or less inoperative as sources of mediation between elites and non- elites. As a result, large numbers of people are available for mass appeals, as evidenced in the success of communism, Gaullism, and Poujadism in recent years. Since World War II no other Western democracy has witnessed such wide- spread mass attacks on the constitutional order. More than one hundred years ago, De Tocqueville also argued that French political upheavals were related to the lack of inde-

---

29. See Rose (1954, pp. 105-6, 110, 112). Cf. Mannheim's statement: "France, too, has the smaller cities and the provinces as counter-forces to pro- tect it against the mechanisms of mass society" (1940, p. 88); and Luethy's statement: "The empty and impoverished life of most French villages and provincial towns, whose monuments bear witness to a former vitality, is the result of [the centralization of French society]" (1957, p. 20).

30. Charles Bettleheim and S. Frère, *Une Ville Française Moyenne: Auxerre en 1950*, p. 282 (cited in Rose, 1954, p. 75).

pendent group life; and over fifty years ago Durkheim stated
his belief that France suffered from the paucity of what he
called "secondary groups" intermediate between state and
individual:

Our political malaise thus has the same origin as the social
malaise we are suffering from. It too is due to the lack of secondary organs intercalated between the State and the rest of the
society. We have already seen that these organs seem necessary
to prevent the State from tyrannizing over individuals; it is now
plain that they are equally essential to prevent individuals from
absorbing the State. They liberate the two confronted forces,
whilst linking them at the same time. We can see how serious
this lack of internal organization is, which we have noted so
often: this is because it involves in fact something of a profound
loosening and an enervation, so to speak, of our whole social
and political structure. The social forms that used to serve as a
framework for individuals and a skeleton for the society, either
no longer exist or are in course of being effaced, and no new
forms are taking their place. So that nothing remains but the
fluid mass of individuals. For the State itself has been reabsorbed
by them. Only the administrative machine has kept its stability
and goes on operating with the same automatic regularity.
(Durkheim, 1958, p. 106)

Germany appears to be similar to France and different
from England and the United States in respect to the development of multiple independent groups that participate
in the direction of public affairs. In a recent study of West
German society, the author described the crucial differences between Germany, on the one side, and England and
the United States, on the other, as follows:

In Germany, there is a sharp break between the public and the
private spheres. Political and social responsibility is an attribute
of office, whether in the parliaments, the ministries, the churches,
the trade-unions, or the interest-groups. What is more, within
these various political structures a strong hierarchical spirit dominates, so that political responsibility and communication tend
to be confined to the very heights of these institutions. In
England and the United States, on the other hand, there is a
gradation from public to private. Private association for public

purposes is not confined to political parties and interest-groups, but includes a variety of general and special public-interest groups concerned with policy issues of all kinds at all levels of the governmental process. Power and communication are more or less decentralized within these organizations. . . . The shortcomings of democratic society in Germany result from absence of such institutional pluralism. (Almond, 1957, pp. 238-9)

France and Germany suffer from the failure to have developed and sustained an intermediate structure of independent groups. The centralization of national organization is one major consequence. Conversely, whenever there is expropriation of major social functions by large organizations, smaller groups lose their reasons for existence (except perhaps as administrative agencies). This loss of function, in turn, undermines the meaning smaller groups possess for their participants. No group can lose its character-defining functions and remain a source of meaning and belonging. An organization whose performance falls far short of its avowed purposes loses meaning: the subjective response of the individual is tied to the objective role of the group. Thus, the role of local organization becomes attenuated as decision-making and communication shift toward a national center, with the consequence that rank and file members find little basis for participation in it. Similarly, the role of a job in the fashioning of a product becomes attenuated as that job becomes increasingly subdivided and removed from the worker's control, with the consequence that the individual finds little basis for a sense of workmanship and status in it.[31] In like manner, as the role of the local community in leisure activities progressively gives way to the national media of entertainment, the individual finds less to interest him in his community.[32] In sum, the attenua-

31. Of the voluminous literature on the alienation of labor, the writings of Karl Marx are especially noteworthy (n. d., pp. 395-400, 708-9). See also Fromm (1953, pp. 125-31, 177-84) and Arendt (1958, pp. 248-57).

32. On the alienation of leisure, see Fromm (1953, pp. 131-7) and Riesman (1953, pp. 315-45).

tion of association, occupation, and community characterizes
the intermediate structure of mass society.

Isolation of Personal Relations

Personal as well as intermediate relations become increasingly peripheral to the central operations of the mass
society. This is shown by the change in social position of
the family from an extended kinship system to an *isolated*
conjugal unit following upon the loss of many social functions. The family gives up its educational role to a public
school system, its mutual aid role to a social security system,
and so on. The loss of functions sharply limits the public
meaning of the family, though not necessarily its private
meaning, and diminishes its capacity for relating the individual to the larger society. Kinship units may be too narrow in scope and too far removed from the public realm to
be able to provide an effective basis for developing interest
and participation in it.

With this argument in mind, many students of mass
society imply that mass society lacks family ties as well
as intermediate social relations. This view is open to
serious question. In the first place, since the family by itself
is inherently incapable of linking the individual to large-
scale society, it is theoretically unnecessary to assume that
such relations are absent in order to have a mass society.
In other words, it is entirely possible to have a society in
which there are family ties but which is still a mass
society due to the lack of intermediate relations. Furthermore, since the individual who is *totally* isolated (that
is, without even family ties) for long periods is not
likely to possess that minimum of personal organization required by collective activity, the loss of all family life leads
to personal deviance—in the extreme case, mental disorders

and suicides—rather than to mass behavior. But it is mass behavior which marks the mass society.

Data showing that extreme personal deviance and extreme political behavior do not vary together lend support to this view, for they indicate that different social conditions may give rise to each. Thus, if the proportion of the electorate which supports the Communist party may be taken as an indicator of the extent of extremist political behavior in a society, and if the proportion of the population recorded as suicides, manslayers, and alcoholics may be used as indicators of the extent of personal deviance in a society, then it may be shown that countries characterized by relatively strong Communist movements are not generally characterized by relatively high rates of personal deviance; and, conversely, countries with relatively small Communist electorates do not tend to have relatively low rates of personal deviance. More precisely, if Australia, Canada, Denmark, Finland, France, Italy, Norway, Sweden, Switzerland, United Kingdom, and United States are ranked by size of the Communist vote in the first election after 1949, and if they are ranked by proportion of suicides in 1949, *the rank order correlation between suicide rate and Communist vote is —.26.* If the same countries are ranked according to rate of homicides rather than suicides, *the rank order correlation between proportion of manslayers and of Communist voters is —.08.* If these countries are ranked by proportion of alcoholics and of Communist voters, the correlation is —.38.[33] We may conclude that there is *no evidence here for a positive relation between conditions that favor mass deviance and those that favor personal deviance.* If anything, there may be a slight negative relation, since all three coefficients are negative.

---

33. Statistics on suicide, homicide, and alcoholism are from Fromm (1953, pp. 8-9). Canada and the United Kingdom are not included in the correlation of alcoholics and Communist vote, because data on number of alcoholics were not given.

The same conclusion is reached when we compare changes in the suicide rate with changes in the Communist vote *within each country*. Comparing the direction of change in the per cent Communist vote with the direction of change in the crude suicide rate for each pair of election years in twelve European countries between 1921 and 1954,[34] we find that they change in *opposite* directions in 36 out of the 60 comparisons, or 60% of the time. In only two out of the twelve countries do the two measures change in the same direction (increase or decrease together) in a majority of cases. The following observations on the social conditions underlying support of communism in Sweden are consistent with these data.

The kind of social isolation which is associated with Communist voting behavior is ordinarily not caused by individual maladjustment. *Those who vote Communist usually seem to have satisfactory primary group relations in the home, factory, and community.* Furthermore, the suicide rate in Sweden is not positively correlated with the Communist vote. Suicides are least frequent in the "reddest" county. (Davison, 1954-55, p. 378; italics added)

Thus, there are good theoretical and empirical reasons (although the data are far from conclusive) for not assuming that the loss of family life is a necessary condition underlying mass tendencies. Rather, we contend that it is the *isolation* of the family and other primary groups which marks the mass society.

Since social isolation, as the term will be used herein, refers to the lack of social relations to the larger society, individuals may be isolated even though they possess family ties—so long as the family groups in turn are not linked to the larger society in any firm way. For isolated families (or other kinds of primary associations, such as friendship groups) cannot by themselves provide the basis for understanding or managing the impersonal environment with which the individual also must grapple. Therefore, whereas

---

34. Suicide data are from World Health Organization (1956, pp. 250-53).

the isolation of a small group does not entail the isolation of its members from one another, the individual member of such a group may nevertheless be isolated from the common life of the "great society." A central proposition of this study states that meaningful and effective participation in the larger society requires a structure of groups intermediate between the family and the nation; and the weakness of such a structure creates a vulnerability to mass movements. Participation in small but isolated groups such as the family is no substitute for participation in intermediate groups and may even be favorable to participation in mass movements, since the individual is more likely to engage in new ventures when he receives support from his close associates, and because the member of even a small group is a more accessible target for mass agitation than is a completely unattached person. In other words, the totally isolated individual (that is, the person without *any* social ties) will be unable to maintain his personal organization sufficiently to engage in cooperative ventures of any kind, whereas the individual who has personal ties but no broader ties in the society is more likely to be available for mass movements.[35]

Centralization of National Relations

The organizing principle of large-scale mass society centers on the national level. This is indicated by the proliferation of governmental functions in previously autonomous spheres of activity, by the growth of national organizations, and by the concomitant shift in power from local to national centers. Structures on the national level develop in response to the size and complexity of society; they expropriate functions formerly reserved to intermediate

35. For further discussion of this point, see Part III, pp. 217-18 below.

groups and the family. Modern mass society is characterized by the great degree to which this transference has taken place, so that the state and national organization assume the central role in the direction of all kinds of collective activity. Mass society finds a major basis of integration in large-scale organization. Therefore, we would be misconstruing mass society if we were to describe it as a state of social disorganization.

National organization that is centralized at the expense of smaller forms of association helps to create amorphous masses. People are more easily manipulated and mobilized when they become directly and exclusively dependent on the national organization for the satisfaction of interests otherwise also met in proximate relations. When the national organization is atomized, its members find it increasingly difficult to orient themselves to the larger society. They cannot understand the workings of the overall system, in part because "there are far few positions from which the major structural connections between different activities can be perceived, and fewer men can reach these vantage points" (Mannheim, 1940, p. 59). Furthermore, increasing distance between centers of decision and daily life make it more difficult for people to grasp the meaning of issues at stake. Faced with the impersonality and incomprehensibility of national relations, and at the same time lacking an independent group life, the individual may withdraw from participation in the larger society. Or he may act in spite of the lack of group relations. Certain spheres of mass society are based on such unmediated participation of large numbers of individuals.

Large-scale communication is based on mass participation when it is divorced from intermediate relations, and prevails over other modes that are anchored in such relations. Agencies of large-scale communication are not necessarily mass media, however. They become so when they lose their ties to local and personal forms of communication. Mere growth

STRUCTURE OF MASS SOCIETY

in size of these agencies makes mass relations more probable (but certainly not inevitable), as it encourages national centralization and discourages local relations of those who manage the media.[36] Thus, the genuine community newspaper forms a link in the local chain of gossip and discussion, as its staff members participate in face-to-face relations with their readers. By contrast, the mass media lack such intermediate associations; as a result, instead of sharing a community of value and interest with their audience, they substitute organizational and market relations on a national level.

In general, formal organizations are to be identified as mass organizations, not by their size, but when they lack intermediate units which have some autonomy from the central leadership. In the absence of a structure of smaller groups, formal organizations themselves become remote from their members. That is, they get beyond the reach of their members, and as a result cannot deeply influence them nor command their allegiance in the face of competition for member loyalties. Consequently, members of excessively bureaucratized organizations may become mobilized by totalitarian elites. This is illustrated by the Nazi success in capturing many youth groups in Germany during the 1920's.

Prior to World War I, Germany witnessed a great upsurge of youth movements, filled with young men and women who were alienated from existing religion, politics, business, education, art, literature, and family life. The youth movements themselves were "at bottom random,' 'goalless,' but persistent attempts to replace the crumbled value system . . . with another which would in some way focus the longing for a sacred experience" (Becker, 1946, p. 51). But the pre-war youth movement sank into routine in the early

36. The change in the *Manchester Guardian,* a leading English newspaper, has been considered in this light (Taylor, 1957, p. 12). "The *Manchester Guardian* . . . has ceased to represent Manchester except in name . . . it is now a national paper pure and simple. . . . The London office provides most of the paper. . . . Now the editor plays little part in local politics."

1920's. Esoteric and intimate aspects of the movement became commonplace. The initially spontaneous charismatic leadership grew matter-of-fact and even traditional. The tendency toward tutelage by adults created centralized and routinized office staffs for many youth organizations. The whole movement became bureaucratized. Hitler, Goebbels, and Rosenberg seized the opportunity to exploit the widespread yearning for action on the part of both leaders and members of the youth movements. By 1923, the Nazis proclaimed the establishment of the Greater German Youth Movement to capture these restive youths. Funds were appropriated for an intensive propaganda campaign. By the end of 1924, Nazi youth groups were shooting up throughout Upper Saxony. After Hitler announced the creation of the Hitler Youth as a party auxiliary at the 1926 party convention, the organization spread rapidly (Becker, 1946, pp. 145-6).

Members or clients of an organization who are alienated from the leadership are favorite targets for mass movements. Communist successes among unemployed trade unionists in England during the depression have been related to the lack of close ties between the central Trade Union Congress and the local Trades Councils. In the absence of effective communication and organic bonds, the national leadership was insufficiently responsive to the distress of its members, with the result that the local organizations "were left without either lead or help from the centre and were thus easily led to back the Communists" (Cole, 1948, p. 148). Communist (and Nazi) penetration of the unemployed ranks in Germany likewise was facilitated by poor relations between trade union leadership and the ranks, in this instance in part because union functions were being absorbed by the state. German trade union connections with the workers were "unquestionably weakened by the increased activity of the state in the regulation of wages and conditions of unemployment." The vast array of economic functions administered by the state induced workers to believe they no longer needed unions (F. Neumann, 1936, pp. 31-2). At the same time rank and file members were becoming less and less committed to their unions, the leadership of both the trade unions and the Social Democratic party was becoming more and more entrenched and entwined in the government apparatus (Schorske, 1955, pp. 127-8). As a result, there developed "an increasing gap between what the average worker hoped and expected, and what was being said and done by the reformist, government-affiliated bureaucracy of the SPD and the unions" (Kirchheimer, 1957, p. 138). Membership in the socialist unions declined, and, especially as unemployment rose, both the Communists and the Nazis won increasing working-class support.

When, on the other hand, unions have developed strong locals, clubs, and the like, which perform important economic and social functions for their members, these members possess multiple relations to the organization, and to the larger social order—commitments they are not likely to endanger by supporting extremist movements. A study of the International Typographical Union shows how independent subgroup formation not only ties printers to the union, but also how it facilitates democratic processes within it (Lipset et al., 1956). The I.T.U. is perhaps the most democratic union in America. Its distinguishing feature is a permanent two-party system, which guarantees an ever-present source of criticism of and alternative leadership to the incumbent administration. The two parties are not the only independent groups within the union to relate the rank and file and leadership, however. In addition, and supportive of the party-system as well as the union, there are strong and relatively autonomous locals, large enough to protect their members from undue outside coercion, and small enough to provide an interpersonal basis for participation in the union's affairs. Furthermore, the printers possess a flourishing "occupational community," organized around a plurality of independent benevolent organizations, newspapers, athletic teams, lodges, social clubs, and informal relations. Although these subgroups are not part of the union, nor explicitly political in any way, they serve to increase political participation in the union (for example, by increasing contact of non-political printers with those who already are active in union politics), to train new union leaders (especially as a result of filling their own leadership needs for club officials), and to give their members a greater stake in maintaining the social order of the occupation, including the union and its party system. In short, through parties, locals, clubs, and friendships, as well as a result of other factors (such as the insulation of the printing occupation from other manual trades), printers develop multiple ties to their work, their union, and the larger social order of which they are a part.

Nisbet argues that unless all kinds of large-scale organizations are rooted in partially autonomous subgroups, they intensify rather than counteract the process of atomization:

> The labor union, the legal or medical association, or the church will become as centralized and as remote as the national State itself unless these great organizations are rooted in the smaller relationships which give meaning to the ends of the large associations. . . . Only thus will the large formal associations remain important agencies of order and freedom in democracy. (Nisbet, 1953, p. 277)

Large-scale organizations that fail to develop or sustain independent subgroups tend to be characterized by low levels of membership participation. Because they are not close enough to their members to allow for effective participation, mass organizations engender widespread apathy. Furthermore, the lack of a pluralist structure within organizations, like its absence in the larger society, not only discourages membership participation. It also discourages the formation of an informed membership, the development of new leadership, and the spread of responsibility and authority, so that the wide gap between the top and the bottom of mass organizations tends to be bridged by manipulation.[37]

At the same time that mass relations permit extensive manipulation of people by elites, they also encourage manipulation of elites by non-elites. Elites are more directly influenced by non-elites in the absence of intermediate groups because they are less insulated. Elites lose their insulation since demands and impulses of large numbers of people that formerly were sublimated and fulfilled by intermediate groups now are focused directly on the national level. Higher elites absorb functions formerly reserved to intermediate elites and therefore no longer can depend on these groups to siphon off popular pressures and to regulate participation. Furthermore, popular participation in the higher elites is all the stronger and less restrained for being in part a substitute for diversified participation in intermediate groups—especially in times of crisis.

In conclusion, the growth of centralized organizations at the expense of intermediate groups constrains both elites and non-elites to engage in efforts to directly manipulate the other. Media of communication that command the attention of millions of people simultaneously are major instruments of this manipulation by those who command them, but also by the audience upon which their success or failure directly is dependent. Centralized decision-making also may cut two ways: if the populace can make its voice felt more easily when it can influence directly one master decision, rather than having to influence many smaller decisions to achieve the same result, then by the same token elites also may grasp one major lever of power more readily than many smaller ones. Centralization of decision-making functions does not preclude direct intervention either by the mass or the elite, although it certainly does prevent people from expressing and implementing *individual* views on public matters. When

37. Cf. Selznick (1952, p. 290).

centralized national relations are combined with weak intermediate relations and isolated family relations, elites are unprotected from mass pressures and masses are unprotected
from elite pressures. The structure of mass society thus provides extensive opportunity for mass movements. The character of that structure may now be summarized.

Social groups larger than the family and smaller than the
state operate to link elites and non-elites, so that the nature
of these groups shapes the political relation. Where intermediate groups do not exist or do not perform important
social functions, elites and non-elites are directly dependent
on one another: there is non-mediated access to elites and
direct manipulation of non-elites. This kind of social arrangement leaves society vulnerable to anti-democratic movements based on mass support. Centralized national groups
do not mitigate mass availability; neither do isolated primary
groups. For the one relationship is too remote and the other
is too weak to provide the individual with firm bases of
attachment to society. This is the situation of mass society.

Where many social groups are operative, the question is
whether they are autonomous, that is, free from domination
by other groups, and of limited scope, that is, influential
with respect to only limited aspects of their members' lives.
Where groups are influential with respect to the whole of
their members' lives (for example, where "the status of every
man was fixed by his place in some community—manor, bor-
ough, guild, learned University or convent" [Trevelyan,
1953, p. 239]), the political structure tends to be authoritarian but not totalitarian, since each community is to some
degree independent and therefore capable of limiting the
power of a central elite. This is the situation of more complex communal societies, such as medieval society with its
corporations that protected the individual from undue external interference, for example, by the monarchy, but
that did not give him much leeway with respect to the corporate authority itself.

Where, on the other hand, social groups are not only inclusive of their members' lives but also are themselves controlled by a central elite, then the political structure tends to be totalitarian. For in this case the individual is available to the central elite through his intermediate affiliations, which are instituted by the elite precisely for this purpose. Thus, whereas the medieval guild could help prevent the state from easy manipulation of its members by virtue of the guild's independence of the king, the state-dominated trade union is an instrument of the political elite for the mobilization of workers (as in the Soviet Union today). Where the trade union is not only independent of the state, but in addition the worker is not under the domination of his union except with reference to limited areas of life, then it supports a liberal democratic rule. The trade union must fulfill important social functions, however, for otherwise it becomes merely another organization without the ability to define and protect its members' position in the larger society. Intermediate groups whose functions have been absorbed by national structures mark the mass society. A wide variety of independent, limited-function organizations permits democratic control but also insulates both elite and non-elite from undue interference in the life of the other. This is the situation of pluralist society.

Social arrangements may encourage tendencies that transform the political system. This is especially true of the mechanisms of mass society, for they permit an abundance of mass movements. A major objective of this study is to identify the social origins and social bases of mass movements. On the basis of our model of mass society, we expect to find that mass movements are facilitated by the atomization of social relations, since unattached people are disposed to engage in mass action. We shall attempt to show this in Part II and Part III. But before turning to an analysis of the social origins of mass tendencies, we shall briefly consider cultural and psychological properties of mass society.

Chapter 4

Culture and Personality
in Mass Society

A SOCIETY is characterized not only by the nature of its social structure, but also by the quality of its culture and the psychological character of its members. The social relations that distinguish a society tend to acquire *cultural legitimacy* and *psychological support*. This chapter attempts to delineate cultural and psychological properties which distinguish our four types of society, and to suggest how the cultural and psychological properties of mass society fail to provide firm support for democratic institutions.

Cultural Properties
of Mass Society

The lack of a variety of local groups is associated with the lack of a variety of local cultures, and, correlatively, the existence of mass relations is associated with the presence of mass standards. The substitution of mass standards for local cultures increases the availability of the population by loosening the cultural basis for multiple loyalties and by strengthening the legitimacy of the mass. It also increases direct access to elites by devaluing elite standards and the legitimacy of authority. Mass standards, in turn, are readily used by mass-oriented elites as bases for manipulating and mobilizing large numbers of people. Therefore, a society characterized by mass standards lacks strong cultural support for the defense of basic institutions, especially liberal democracy. In order to examine this argument, we first must define mass standards.

Critics of mass culture generally agree that mass standards are *uniform* (i.e., levelled) and at the same time *fluid* (i.e., readily changed).[38] Cultural differentiation requires social differentiation. Since mass society tends to lack a variegated group life, it favors cultural uniformity. This uniformity involves not only a factual levelling of standards; it also becomes *normative*. In politics uniformity receives cultural legitimacy in the guise of *populism*. Primacy is given to "the belief in the intrinsic and immediate validity of the popular will" (Shils, April 1954, p. 103). The uniformity of opinion among large numbers of people becomes the supreme standard, superordinate to traditional values, professional standards, and institutional autonomy. Populism is cause as well as effect in the operation of mass society. The internalization of this belief in the intrinsic and immediate validity of mass opinion prepares people for active service in mass movements seeking to determine policies and personnel for all kinds of institutions. For example, McCarthyism as a mass movement sought to attack policy and personnel of the Army, State Department, *New York Times,* and Harvard University, among other institutions.

Mass standards also are fluid. Whenever standards are set by large numbers of people, they will tend to manifest frequent change in content. When in addition large numbers of people participate in the determination of standards as members of an undifferentiated collectivity (mass), then changes in content are more likely to be discontinuous. For

---

38. See Rosenberg and White (1957) for a representative series of articles on mass culture.

example, standards set according to fashion result from people's actions as members of differentiated social strata, and correspondingly show a continuity in the changes themselves; whereas standards set by people as members of a mass may change abruptly and unpredictably, as in fads and crazes.[39]

Nevertheless, standards set according to mass dispositions may persist as the prevailing design for living of a society, supported by mass organization and in turn sustaining that structure. Mass standards are supported by organizations that treat people as members of an undifferentiated (mass) audience or market. They support mass organization in that they help to form and sustain the mass audience required for commercial success by the mass media of communication, or for political success by the mass party, etc.

This does not mean that a democratic society necessarily produces mass uniformity or widespread demand for political conformity. Democratic society does not have to be associated with severe suppression of cultural variety *so long as equal rights are not confused with the obliteration of all social differences.* Even as rigid class distinctions dissolve with the growth of democracy, other forms of social differentiation often develop along with equalitarianism. Thus, majority rule in politics need not be populistic, so long as people form their political choices as participants in a variety of independent groups. *Social pluralism* engenders *diversity* in culture and politics. At the same time, contact between diverse sub-cultures produces a high rate of change in standards, as people from different cultural worlds are constantly exposed to one another and therefore to diverse and often conflicting standards. Therefore, pluralist society exhibits *fluidity* as well as diversity of value-standards. This fluidity and diversity make it difficult for the pluralist system to achieve *consensus.*

Communal society does not experience major difficulty in achieving consensus, since standards tend to be *fixed* by

---

39. Cf. Turner and Killian (1957, p. 216).

tradition. At the same time, standards are *differentiated* by status, those deemed appropriate for one status (such as the nobility) being different from those which are obligatory for another status (such as the peasantry). However, the fixity of standards in communal society impairs its capacity for innovation and adaptation to new conditions, as when an alien culture impinges on a previously isolated communal system.

Standards also tend to be *fixed* in totalitarian society, since they are set by a political elite that possesses a monopoly of power. In addition, standards are *levelled,* since the population is socially undifferentiated. If standards were not uniform, the elite could not use them to manipulate and mobilize the population.

These different kinds of cultural standards characterizing our four types of society may be diagrammed as follows:

	DIFFERENTIATED STANDARDS	UNIFORM STANDARDS
FIXED STANDARDS	traditionalism	monism
FLUID STANDARDS	pluralism	populism

Comparing this diagram of cultural types with the diagram of types of society, we may infer that atomized masses encourage cultural uniformity, and that accessible elites favor cultural fluidity. When people form a socially differentiated body, they will be more capable of developing standards differentiated according to status and group. And when elites are inaccessible, they will be more capable of preserving fixed standards. However, there is no one-to-one relation between social and cultural differentiation or stability. In the United States, for example, there appears to be greater social differentiation than cultural differentiation, perhaps in part because of the system of popular education that prevails in this country. In France, on the other hand, the reverse situation seems to obtain, in part due to the elitist character of educational institutions in that country.

Having indicated our conception of mass standards, we may return to the problem of their political consequences. By adhering to mass standards, elites and non-elites become increasingly similar. This confounding of functions results from the fundamental direct dependency of each upon the other. The need to appeal directly to certain common bases of response among large numbers of people (as against seeking to line up support by putting together various combinations of interests and groupings) arises from the very presence of the mass. If elites do not cast their appeal to people as members of a nation-wide mass, rather than as members of differentiated groups, they become subject to displacement by counter-elites who do command mass support. If they do cast their appeals to the mass, they become increasingly accessible to manipulation by outside forces. For example, they become susceptible to the demands of those who claim to "speak for" the masses. When this happens, leaders apply to potential allies and participants "only the most superficial tests—those having to do with criteria of technical competence and of agreement on immediate issues" (Selznick, 1952, p. 310), in order to gain contact with the mass. That this provides opportunities for groups with dictatorial ambitions is evident in instances where socialists engage in united action with Communists (such as in Popular Fronts and Unity parties), "a process which has uniformly resulted in subversion of the socialist organizations."

This vulnerability has increased whenever the socialists have lost sight of their relation to the values of the liberal-democratic tradition and have given priority to certain immediate political and economic aims in such a way as to permit collaboration with anyone who supported those aims. (Selznick, 1952, p. 311)

A parallel failure to sustain a political identity as a result of the substitution of opportunistic considerations for central values is to be found in the collaboration of German conservatives with the Nazi movement. A leading German conservative who himself collaborated with the Nazis has analyzed this failure.

To begin with, it must be recalled that the world of ideas of the nationalist, conservative, and liberal middle class and aristocracy, and of the intellectuals, had long been invaded by scepticism. The whole of these "ruling" classes, no less than the mass of the proletariat of the great towns, had been moving towards nihilism. They had even been moving faster in that direction than the working class. Faith in traditions had been fading, faith in machinery and devices and materialism had been growing, among the traditional ruling classes, and had turned them from opponents into allies of National Socialism. The absence of doctrine is perhaps the strength of the [Nazis]; the absence of tradition in the monarchist and conservative elements is certainly their weakness. (Rauschning, 1939, p. 100)

When certain leading conservatives themselves became convinced of the need to organize masses and when they entered into coalition with the National Socialists for this purpose, the demise of conservatism in Germany was at hand.

In short, whether socialist or conservative, political groups that substitute mass standards for their own standards lose the capacity to sustain themselves as independent forces. Whenever they lose their own sense of direction, leaders as well as members of political groups are open to capture by mass-oriented elites. "It is this general lack of direction in modern mass society that gives the opportunity to groups with dictatorial ambitions" (Mannheim, 1940, p. 87).

Psychological Properties
of Mass Society

By divorcing people from larger social purposes, mass society also tends to separate people from themselves. An individual who acquires a feeling of social usefulness and social status in the society finds it easier to form a positive conception of himself. An individual who lacks opportunity for participation in society fails to receive support for a sense of his own worth and therefore finds it more difficult to sustain favorable attitudes toward himself. Self-estrangement, in turn, heightens the individual's readiness for activistic "solutions" to the anxiety accompanying personal alienation. For the individual who lacks a firm conception of himself and confidence in himself does not possess the basis for strong control over himself, and therefore is highly *suggestible* to appeals emanating from remote places. Members of elites as well as non-elites may become self-alienated and suggestible, with the consequence that they are readily attracted to mass movements.

Critics of the mass man generally agree that this psychological type is self-estranged: "[He] does not experience himself as the active bearer of his own powers and richness, but as an impoverished 'thing' dependent on powers outside of himself, unto whom he has projected his living substance" (Fromm, 1955, p. 124).[40] The separation of the individual (and his family) from major social processes and cultural values tends to separate the individual from himself. Thus, people who feel alienated from the social order tend to feel alienated from themselves.

A study of auto workers shows that individuals who feel socially alienated (as indicated by a lack of confidence in other people and in the future) also tend to feel personally impotent, at least with regard to political matters. If we may use feelings of personal impotence in political matters as an indicator of self-alienation, then these data may be interpreted as showing that auto workers who feel divorced from their fellows also tend to feel a lack of confidence in themselves (Kornhauser *et al.*, 1956, p. 194).[41]

---

40. On the psychological character of the individual in mass society, see also Fromm (1941); Riesman (1953); Hoffer (1951); and Bettelheim (1955).
41. The table reports only the extremes, omitting intermediate percentages.

POLITICAL FUTILITY	SOCIAL ALIENATION	
	High	Low
High	60%	12%
Low	9	56

A high proportion of the socially alienated workers also express self-alienation in their low sense of personal accomplishments, their low estimate of chances for personal improvement, and other indications of personal dissatisfactions (Kornhauser *et al.*, 1956, p. 195).[42]

LIFE-SATISFACTION	SOCIAL ALIENATION	
	High	Low
Low	45%	12%
High	27	37

A characteristic response to estrangement from self is diffuse anxiety and the search for substitute forms of integration. The alienated individual's lack of ego-integration makes him highly susceptible to manipulation. Since in the mass society uniform (mass) opinion is substituted for a diversity of culture-patterns, the individual who is self-alienated is forced to turn to this mass opinion for directives on how to feel about himself. "Instead of looking for gratifications which are in line with his particular personality he accepts those suggested and prepared by the manipulators of the mass media, or of the masses. He can do so only because he no longer feels able to decide autonomously on what suits him best" (Bettelheim, 1955, p. 251). Therefore, the mass man substitutes an undifferentiated image of himself for an individualized one; he answers the perennial question of "Who am I?" with the formula "I am like everyone else."

In pluralist society, on the other hand, the inner cohesion of local groups and cultures provides a firmer basis for self-

---

42. The table reports only the extremes, omitting intermediate percentages.

relatedness, and the diversity of groups and cultures permits the individual to form a distinctive self-image. Social and cultural pluralism invites the development of differentiated, autonomous individuals, for variety in institutions and values encourages the individual to compare different models of conduct and to integrate elements from several models into a distinctive identity. The *autonomous man* respects himself as an individual, experiencing himself as the bearer of his own power and as having the capacity to determine his life and to affect the lives of his fellows. Personal autonomy does not develop apart from society and culture: it requires pluralism in society and culture. Non-pluralist society lacks the diversity of social worlds to nurture and sustain independent persons. Furthermore, in non-pluralist society the man who becomes alienated from the prevailing culture is likely to become alienated from himself; whereas in pluralist society there are alternative loyalties (sanctuaries) which do not place the nonconformist outside the social pale.

In communal society, the individual is constrained to find a satisfactory relation to himself only by conforming to traditional standards and authorities. Hence, the psychological type characteristic of communal society is *tradition-directed* (Riesman, 1953, pp. 24-8). Conformity to tradition provides a basis for acceptance of oneself, but only as a member of the community and not as an individual. "The tradition-directed person . . . hardly thinks of himself as an individual. Still less does it occur to him that he might shape his own destiny in terms of personal, lifelong goals or that the destiny of his children might be separate from that of the family group" (Riesman, 1953, p. 33). Conformity to tradition is a very different sort of psychological pattern from that compliance with mass opinion which marks the relation of the individual to mass society. In the first place, tradition-direction is a basis for self-relatedness, rather than a source of self-alienation. In the second place, adherence to tradition favors group-centered attitudes, rather than self-centered orientations. That is, the traditional man conforms in order to fulfill his obligations to the group, to avoid shame, whereas the mass man conforms for the purpose of over-coming the diffuse *anxiety* which accompanies the lack of self-confidence. The psychologically autonomous is driven more by *guilt* than by either shame or anxiety (Riesman, 1953, pp. 40-2).

Totalitarian society produces a psychological type that is self-alienated, like the mass man, but group-centered, like the tradition-directed person. Totalitarian society engenders this combination by denying any respect to the individual and by attaching all meaning to the group (especially the party in conjunction with the state). Possessing no legitimate privacy and few personalized models of conduct, the indi-vidual in totalitarian society sheds an unwanted sense of individuality and submits psychologically as well as be-haviorally to the group. He does not regard himself as distinct from the group. Since the group is dominated by an elite possessed of a monopoly of power, submersion in the group entails submission to the elite. Extreme submission to the elite and extreme hostility toward outsiders are characteristic of the *totalitarian man*.[43]

These psychological types may be summarized in the following fashion:

	SELF-RELATED	SELF-ALIENATED
GROUP-ORIENTED	traditional man	totalitarian man
SELF-ORIENTED	autonomous man	mass man

Our four types of society can be differentiated according to the predominance of one or another mechanism by which people regulate their own and others' conduct: honor and shame in communal society, suggestibility and anxiety in

43. Cf. Adorno *et al.* (1950); Fromm (1941); Shils (1954). Shils's work is especially valuable for its stress on the character traits common to both Fascist and Communist activists.

mass society, self-reliance and guilt in pluralist society, sub-missiveness and fear in totalitarian society.

Comparing the psychological types with the types of society, we may infer that firm social relations favor firm relations to self, and that open (accessible) institutions en-courage individualism. But when people constitute an un-differentiated mass, each finds it difficult to form and sustain a stable personal identity. And when social groups (especially elites) are closed, there is little opportunity for people to develop the idea that the state and society are conditions and means for individual well-being, rather than ends in them-selves.

The psychological type characteristic of mass society pro-vides little support for liberal democratic institutions. The mass man clearly is available for mobilization by mass movements, since he lacks a strong set of internalized standards and substitutes standards of the mass. There-fore, in the absence of an acceptable self-image, the indi-vidual seeks to overcome the anxiety accompanying self-alienation by apathy or activism. Withdrawal from activity and flight into activity are both responses characteristic of the mass man. The activistic response underlies much of the participation in mass movements, as individuals seek to substitute external identities for inner ones, to re-place an unwanted or unknown self with a collective image. Thus the mass man is vulnerable to the appeal of mass movements which offer him a way of overcoming the pain of self-alienation by shifting attention away from himself and by focusing it on the movement.

Participation in mass movements tends to involve sub-mission to a leader and ideology on the one hand and hostility toward the outside world, on the other. Thus the individual who previously sought psychological sustenance in the un-organized mass may now seek to attach himself to a mass-oriented elite and an organized movement. This is to say that whereas the mass man is not totalitarian, he readily may become so. However, just as mass society may contain many anti-democratic movements, even as its dominant organization is not anti-democratic; so mass society may contain many totalitarian personalities, even as its dominant psychological type is not totalitarian. Whatever the relative proportion of these two psychological types (totalitarian and mass), their common trait of self-alienation is of primary significance.

In summary, although self-alienation is not confined to mass society, it tends to be widespread and intense in this kind of society. As a result, mass society is psychologically vulnerable to the appeals of mass movements. Whether or not mass tendencies in character and culture will become expressed in mass movements depends primarily on the social structure and the demands events make upon it. The fact that millions of Germans surrendered to the Nazi appeal undoubtedly is related to the economic crises of the 1920's and 1930's, for under such conditions it becomes very difficult for large numbers of people to remain merely as cynical spectators of politics. This is to say that mass society is not capable of putting up a strong defense against revolutionary attacks on the existing order in times of crisis. Crises break down the already precarious structure of mass society, and as a consequence increase the chances for anti-democratic mass movements.

But what kinds of social processes produce a state of the masses in the first place? In Part II we attempt to specify some of these processes, and then consider the role of crises in the *mobilization* of masses against democratic systems.

Summary of Part I

1. The theory of mass society attempts to explain a variety of phenomena, especially high rates of mass behavior. Applied to political phenomena, the theory attempts to describe the kind of social order that is vulnerable to political mass movements.

2. There are two leading versions of the theory of mass society. Each version yields a useful conception of the nature of a system that is vulnerable to mass movements. However, each conception by itself is inadequate. When the two conceptions are combined, a more general and more useful statement of conditions under which there are widespread movements subversive of individual freedom is secured.

a) One conception, which may be called the aristocratic criticism of mass society, states that if elites are not easily accessible (that is, not readily entered and influenced), widespread movements subversive of individual freedom are less likely than if elites are easily accessible.

b) The other conception, which may be termed the democratic criticism of mass society, states that if non-elites possess an independent group life and therefore are not readily available (that is, not easily manipulated and mobilized), widespread movements subversive of individual freedom are less likely than if non-elites are atomized and therefore readily available to elites.

c) A combination of these two conceptions states the conditions for widespread movements subversive of democratic systems: If elites are relatively inaccessible to direct intervention by non-elites and/or if non-elites are relatively unavailable for mobilization by elites, then mass movements are less likely than if elites are readily accessible *and* if non-elites are readily available.

3. The properties of mass society are relations which engender both readily accessible elites and readily available non-elites.

a) The structure of mass society consists in direct elite–non-elite relations by virtue of the paucity of intermediate groups. The lack of intermediate relations leaves institutional elites poorly related to society, and directly accessible to penetration by mass movements. It also leaves non-elites poorly related to society, and directly available for mobilization by mass-oriented elites.

b) Mass culture consists in value-standards which are uniform and fluid. The lack of differentiated and stable norms leaves both elites and non-elites without direction, and vulnerable to mass appeals.

c) The mass man is highly conscious of his separation from others and from self. Self-alienated attitudes heighten the individual's susceptibility to mass appeals. Mass society is characterized by mass men in elites as well as in non-elites, and therefore by the psychological vulnerability of both elites and non-elites to mass appeals.

PART II

SOCIAL SOURCES

OF MASS MOVEMENTS

Chapter 5

Political Vulnerability
of Mass Society

ARISTOCRATIC and democratic critics of mass society agree that individual freedom is threatened by the growth of mass relations even as they differ on the nature of these relations. Aristocratic theorists diagnose mass society as a state of decline in authority, with the lack of traditional restraints on the popular exercise of power that this implies. They generally believe that mass society invites dictatorship based on mass support.[1] Since popular democracy stirs large numbers of previously quiescent people into action, aristocratic critics judge it to be a cause of popular dictatorship. Therefore, they fear all equalitarian tendencies that thrust large numbers of formerly passive people into the public realm. Such participation, aristocratic critics allege, results in the loss of that exclusiveness of elites which is required for the creative and value-sustaining functions with which they are charged. This excess of participation results from doctrines and practices that replace pre-established status distinctions and prerogatives with universal criteria of participation. The transformation from minority rule to popular sovereignty undermines the hierarchical structure of society,

---

1. See F. Neumann (1957, pp. 236-43) for a discussion of dictatorship based on mass support, which he terms "caesaristic dictatorship" to distinguish it from "simple dictatorship—whether it be military or bureaucratic, the rule of a junta, a caudillo, or even an absolute monarchy" (p. 236).

and thereby leaves masses unrestrained. In short, aristocratic critics see equalitarianism as the primary factor both in undermining the insulation of elites, and in permitting the rise of mass movements destructive of individual liberty: "The democratising of Europe," Nietzsche wrote, "is at the same time an involuntary arrangement for the rearing of tyrants" (quoted by Viereck, 1956, p. 169).

Democratic critics reject the idea that equalitarian tendencies *per se* result in a mass society: "The masses, contrary to prediction [of aristocratic critics], did not result from growing equality of condition . . ." (Arendt, 1951, p. 310). According to many of these theorists, mass society is produced by the growth of large cities and bureaucratic organization, rather than by equalitarianism. For, it is argued, these structural trends deprive people of the social bases of involvement and control in the social order. The growth of the metropolis atomizes community and the growth of bureaucracy thrusts decision-making centers beyond the effective range of understanding and influence, leaving only the isolated and exposed individual. Mills expresses this belief that "the mass society . . . is largely a metropolitan society":

The growth of the metropolis, segregating men and women into narrowed routines and environments, causes them to lose any firm sense of their integrity as a public. The members of publics in smaller communities know each other more or less fully, because they meet in the several aspects of the total life routine. The members of masses in a metropolitan society know one another only as fractions in specialized milieux. . . . In every major area of life, the loss of a sense of structure and the submergence into powerless milieux is the cardinal fact. . . . This loss of any structural view or position is the decisive meaning of the lament over the loss of community. In the great city, the division of milieux and of segregating routines reaches the point of closest contact with the individual and the family, for, although the city is not the unit of prime decision, even the city cannot be seen as a total structure by most of its citizens. (1956, pp. 320-2)

In short, democratic critics generally believe that the specialization and centralization of urban-industrial society are the primary factors in undermining self-governing communities, and in encouraging the growth of elite-domination.

It is evident that these two views of mass society may be distinguished by their relative concern for the protection of authority, on the one hand, and community, on the other. Correspondingly, one view locates the major threat to freedom in equalitarianism, and the other in urbanism-industrialism. Now the difficulties of both these views are immediately apparent. Some relatively democratic societies exhibit pronounced mass movements (e.g., France); others do not (e.g., England). It also is clear that there are marked variations in the extent of mass tendencies displayed by urban-industrial societies; England, for example, is more highly urbanized than the United States but is prey to less mass behavior and fewer mass movements. Our problem, then, is to specify more accurately the conditions under which these processes are associated with the rise of mass movements, and the conditions under which they are not so related. But before turning to this task, which constitutes the major objective in Part II, it is necessary to clarify the relation between the rise of mass movements and the threat to freedom.

Aristocratic and democratic critics alike believe that mass society is *vulnerable to totalitarianism,* rather than to traditional forms of dictatorship. De Tocqueville suggested the distinctive vulnerability of mass society long before the rise of nazism and communism. He wrote:

I think, then, that the species of oppression by which democratic nations are menaced is unlike anything that ever before existed in the world. . . . I seek in vain for an expression that will accurately convey the whole of the idea I have formed of it; the old words *despotism* and *tyranny* are inappropriate: the thing itself is new. (Quoted by Talmon, 1952, p. v)

A recent critic of mass society has written that modern

totalitarianism is a "dictatorship resting on popular enthusiasm and is thus completely different from absolute power wielded by a divine-right King, or by a usurping tyrant" (Talmon, 1952, p. 6). Lederer (1940) and Arendt (1951) in particular have argued that mass society is threatened by totalitarianism. They imply that mass society prevents the development of genuinely authoritarian as well as libertarian forms of rule, since even authoritarianism as an institution involves *limited,* if concentrated, power.[2]

Mass movements against democracy must be sharply distinguished from traditional movements against democracy. Not all anti-democratic ideologies are mass-oriented. Monarchical parties—for example, the PNM in Italy—are not mass movements. Nor in general are the aristocratic parties of Europe, such as the pre-Nazi Conservatives in Germany. This kind of predominantly upper-class resistance to democracy is very different from mass movements against democracy, epitomized by fascism in Italy and nazism in Germany, as well as by Communist movements wherever they develop. These mass movements are characteristically *populistic* attacks on democratic institutions and constitutional liberty. They are profoundly revolutionary since they seek to abrogate all institutional restraints on political power, rather than to reinstate some form of aristocratic or theocratic rule.

The decline of community and association creates the opportunity for mass movements to smash all institutional restraints on power and to transform the scope of power. Thus, while totalitarianism is a dictatorship based on mass support, and while it is also based on elite-domination of centralized organization, its distinctive character lies in the

---

2. Arendt (1956) argues that many a liberal notes the decline of liberty and cries totalitarianism; and many a conservative measures the decline of authority and errs equally if he equates this with totalitarianism. She goes on to say that certainly liberty has been threatened, and certainly authority has declined, but totalitarianism may not be equated with either. Totalitarianism, unlike authoritarianism, is not bound to any laws or codes; and unlike ordinary dictatorships or tyrannies, rests not upon parties but *movements* which remain in power even after power has been obtained.

fact that it is a permanently mobilized mass movement which seeks to control all aspects of life. Totalitarian dictatorships involve total domination, limited neither by received laws or codes (as in traditional authoritarianism) nor even by the boundaries of governmental functions (as in classical tyranny), since *they obliterate the distinction between state and society*. Totalitarianism is limited only by the need to keep large numbers of people in a state of constant activity controlled by the elite.

But mass society itself is *not* totalitarian, as we have explained in Part I. It may be transformed into a totalitarian society, however. It is more likely to change in this direction than is either pluralist or communal society. In short, mass society is vulnerable to totalitarianism, even though it is not totalitarian and in any given case may never become so. For mass society possesses only weak defenses against mass-oriented elites who seek to abrogate all restraints on power and raise up new kinds of totalistic ideologies. "It is the mass-oriented elite, Fascist and Communist alike, which is the advocate and engineer of activism" (Selznick, 1952, p. 294). The mass-oriented elite above all distinguishes fascism from ordinary conservatism and communism from democratic socialism. Fascism and communism are extra-ordinary in this sense: they act outside of and in opposition to constitutional order of any kind.

Totalitarian elites strive to create masses as well as to mobilize existing masses. (People cannot be mobilized against the established order until they first have been divorced from prevailing codes and relations.) Only then are they available for "activist modes of intervention" in the political process. Thus it is that when large numbers of people are available, and when opportunities exist for the further creation of mass-consciousness (as when pre-existing elites are inadequate to protect their institutions), Fascist and Communist movements alike gain support at the expense of political parties committed to the social order. Conversely, when such conditions do not obtain, they both lose ground to constitutional forces, as an examination of changes in voting strength of Fascist and Communist parties in several countries shows.

We have been able to identify eight European countries (Austria, Belgium, Denmark, France, Germany, Italy, Norway, Sweden) in which the anti-democratic extremes (communism and fascism) ran candidates in at least two consecutive national elections since 1920. Comparing changes from one election to the next for each country, we find that the Communist and Fascist vote increased or decreased together 16 times out of a total of 24 pairs of elections. In other words, the two anti-democratic extremes changed in the same direction twice as often as they changed in opposite directions. In no country did the two extremes change in opposite directions more often than they changed in the same direction. This pattern gains further significance when we compare changes in the voting strength of each extreme with its democratic counterpart on a left-right continuum. Out of 54 pairs of elections the Communist and socialist vote changed in *opposite* directions 34 times, or in 63% of the cases; and in only one country did the democratic left and the anti-democratic left increase or decrease together more often than not. The results for the right are even more striking: out of 24 pairs of elections the Fascist and the democratic right[3] changed in opposite directions 17 times, or in 71% of the cases. We may infer that changes in conditions that favor one anti-democratic extreme also favor the other, that changes that weaken one extreme also weaken the other, and that changes in conditions affect the democratic parties in the opposite direction from their effect on the political extremes. This suggests that, in spite of important differences between them, anti-democratic mass movements spring from similar social conditions.

---

3. We have included in the "democratic right" all parties standing between the democratic left (especially socialist parties) and the extreme right (especially Fascist parties), hence parties of the "center" as well as of the "right."

What are these conditions? The major set of circumstances associated with the emergence and development of mass movements must include those factors that weaken social arrangements intermediate between the individual and the state. This much is suggested by the structure of mass society. Such factors are those associated with *major discontinuities in social process* as measured by the rate, scope, and mode of social change. Thus, it is not democratization *per se* which produces extremist mass movements, but the discontinuities in political authority that may accompany the introduction of popular rule. Where the pre-established political authority is highly autocratic, rapid and violent displacement of that authority by a democratic regime is highly favorable to the emergence of extremist mass movements that tend to transform the new democracy in antidemocratic directions. Likewise, it is not the growth of urban-industrial organization *per se* that induces mass tendencies, but the discontinuities in community that may be associated with urbanization and industrialization. Where the pre-established community consists of small homogeneous units, rapid urbanization and industrialization are highly favorable to extremist mass movements.

All of these discontinuities are likely to involve major impairment of intermediate relations. Intermediate relations are especially fragile because participation in them often is *voluntary*, they generally lack control over the means of coercion possessed by the state, and they lack the bonds of intimacy possessed by the family. Depending on voluntary participation, and lacking the more permanent and organic qualities of family and state, intermediate relations are less adaptable to major discontinuities in social conditions.

A reconsideration of the two approaches to the genesis of mass tendencies may show that part of the difference between them is a product of different starting points (contexts) and, correspondingly, of different intermediate structures with which they are concerned. The aristocratic critics are committed to some version of a status society, and it is that which they are concerned to preserve against the encroachment of democracy, even when the latter is pluralist. That they nevertheless help to locate the sources of mass society is due to the fact that democratization sometimes is more a process of tearing down the old social order than it is a process of building up a new order.

A society having a traditional system of authority is greatly in need of social formations which can bridge the transition to a new (therefore as yet non-traditional) system of democratic power. Otherwise, no group is able to influence deeply the collective activity; and instead of new values being built into the social structure, there is merely a cultural vacuum and social atomization. Equalitarianism can mean the negation of authority and community, as De Tocqueville saw, even though it also can mean a new kind of authority and community. The aristocratic critics of mass society do not err when they insist on the potential tradition-eroding and fragmenting effects of democratization, so long as their context is held in view. A pluralist context is another matter.

Starting from a pluralist premise, democratic critics proceed to locate the emergence of mass tendencies, not in status-eroding processes, since pluralist society is not status-bound, but in group-eroding processes, since pluralist society rests on a rich and diversified group life. Their worry is that access to power will be closed off, since they begin with an open system and are committed to sustaining it. Therefore, democratic critics focus on the threat of growing specialization and centralization of organization to participation and control through the local community and association.

A difference related to that of context is the kind of intermediate structure which each view stresses. Not all intermediate structures are equally critical safeguards against mass tendencies. Those are critical which in the given context are, or have been, major bases of cohesion. It is only natural, therefore, that the aristocratic and democratic approaches, which took shape in different centuries, should identify the dissolution of different kinds of social formations as the major potential source of masses. In the nineteenth century European context, given the feudal heritage, status groups were critical, such that the failure to develop new forms of association to replace them was potentially mass-producing. But in the twentieth century, and especially in America (since it never had a feudal past and hence no fixed hierarchy of status groups),[4] interest groups and other kinds of voluntary association have been more important, and the dissolution of this kind of group life a greater source of mass tendencies. Writing in the nineteenth century, De Tocqueville emphasized the indispensability of new forms of association where *aristocracies* are lost or absent.

In aristocratic nations the body of the nobles and the wealthy are in themselves natural associations which check the abuses of power. In countries where such associations do not exist, if private individuals cannot create an artificial and temporary substitute for them I can see no permanent protection against the most galling tyranny; and a great people may be oppressed with impunity by a small fraction or by a single individual. (1945, v. I, p. 195)

Writing in the twentieth century, Mills also emphasized the importance of private associations for freedom. But now the problem is defined not as the threat to freedom arising from the failure to develop substitutes for status groups, but as the threat arising from the failure to *preserve* old forms of (private) association in the face of the growth of bureaucratic organization.

The executive ascendancy in economic, military, and political institutions has lowered the effective use of all those voluntary associations which operate between the state and the economy on the one hand, and the family and the individual in the primary group on the other. . . . Such associations are replaced

4. See Hartz (1955).

in virtually every sphere of life by centralized organizations. (1956, pp. 306, 310)

Finally, it should be clear that the kinds of discontinuities in intermediate relations which have been discussed are usually *not* productive of mass movements in totalitarian contexts. Totalitarian elites destroy independent groups and change intermediate relations which they control (for example, the organization and membership of the totalitarian party), without thereby creating opportunities for the rise of new mass movements. On the contrary, totalitarian elites seek to keep the population in an atomized state by means of perpetual and unpredictable change, such as forced migrations, terror, and purge, in order to prevent the formation of independent movements.[5] Deliberate atomization is a technique of total domination. Thus, in the totalitarian society there are masses—created, nurtured, and mobilized by the elite—but there are no independent mass movements.

In summary, major discontinuities in social process produce mass movements by destroying pre-established intermediate relations and by preventing the formation of new associations aligned with the social order. Chapter 6 considers discontinuous modes of democratization of authority, and their mass-producing effects. Chapter 7 shows how rapid rates of urbanization and industrialization initially atomize the community and thereby encourage mass movements. Chapter 8 treats sudden breakdowns in social systems, such as occur during severe depressions and military defeats, and the manner in which they summon mass movements.

---

5. See Brzezinski (1955).

Chapter 6

Discontinuities
in Authority

IN THE transition to democratic government, the question is whether the social formations exist to support authority as well as liberty. Where democratization proceeds without adequate safeguards for authority, it leaves the new rule naked before mass movements which would destroy it. Where democratization proceeds without adequate protection for liberty, it leaves individuals naked before mass-oriented elites which would dominate them. Unless democratic processes can be combined with stable and limited authority, they will favor mass movements subversive of liberty and of democracy itself.

Aristocratic critics of mass society have held out little hope for a stable system of authority in a thorough-going democracy. As a consequence, they believe that liberty and equality are incompatible.[6] For liberty depends on stable authority, and political equality is thought to undermine the legitimacy of authority. In order to remain stable and viable, authority must be grounded in tradition and religion, specifically in a constitutional tradition and in a "higher order" of moral law. Ortega has written in this connection that by committing himself to a rule of law,

6. In this connection Irving Babbitt has written that the "attempt to combine freedom with equality led, and, according to Lord Acton, always will lead, to terrorism" (1924, p. 127).

this individual bound himself to maintain a severe discipline over himself. Under the shelter of liberal principles and the rule of law, minorities could live and act. . . . Today we are witnessing the triumphs of a hyperdemocracy in which the mass acts directly, outside the law, imposing its aspirations and its desires by means of material pressure. (1932, pp. 17-8)

Democratic critics, on the other hand, stress the opposition between liberty and authority, and consequently the need to restrain and limit authority. Furthermore, they assert that liberty without democracy means merely the protection of the privileges of the few. *Democracy is essentially an institutional procedure for changing leadership by free competition for the popular vote.* The existence of free competition for leadership does not necessarily guarantee liberty, but in its absence there is less chance for liberty—especially freedom of expression and association.[7]

At the same time, democratic critics agree that liberty requires restraints on popularly-elected leaders, as well as on minorities, so that the individual is protected from undue and arbitrary coercion by the state. These restraints are provided by a plurality of more or less equal and independent groups which check and balance one another's power. In this manner, no one class (such as an aristocracy) rules society; nor does the state possess unlimited power, since it contains within itself not only a system of constitutional checks and balances (e.g., separation of powers), but also a system of social checks and balances (e.g., representatives of conflicting interest groups).[8] Unless there is democratic rule (in the sense of popular choice among competing candidates for leadership), there is insufficient control over minorities (aristocratic or otherwise) to protect liberty. But unless there is constitutional rule, backed by a system of social checks and balances, minorities are not protected from

7. See Schumpeter (1947, pp. 269-73).

8. See "The Federalist No. 51" (1941, pp. 335-41) on checks and balances. Compare Robert Dahl's critical assessment of Madison's emphasis on constitutional rather than social forms of checks and balances (1956, chap. i).

majorities, nor from the state. Democratic rule, according to this theory, is fully compatible with rule by law so long as the society is *pluralist*. A pluralist society supports a *liberal democracy*, whereas a mass society supports a *populist democracy*.

Pluralist society is liberal in that its social constitution limits power to certain circumscribed areas, and provides opportunities to challenge (through due process of law, freedom of expression, and the like) the manner in which power is exercised. Mass society is not liberal in that its social constitution does not so limit the use of power; even when there are formal restraints on power, their effectiveness is abrogated by the lack of independent groups to protect the individual and the minority from manipulation and coercion. Populist democracy involves *direct action* of large numbers of people, which often results in the circumvention of institutional channels and *ad hoc* invasion of individual privacy. Liberal democracy involves political action mediated by institutional rules, and therefore limitations on the use of power by majorities as well as minorities. The difference between liberal democracy and populist democracy, then, does not concern *who* shall have access to power (in both cases, there is representative rule); rather, it concerns *how* power shall be sought, the mode of access. In liberal democracy the mode of access tends to be controlled by institutional procedures and intermediate associations, whereas in populist democracy the mode of access tends to be more direct and unrestrained.

The possible relations between rule of law and representative rule may be summarized as follows:

REPRESENTATIVE RULE	RULE OF LAW	
	Strong	Weak
Weak	aristocracy	autocracy
Strong	liberal democracy	populist democracy

This diagram can help us to describe two ways in which democracy may develop. Democratic rule introduced where the state is already constitutional tends to develop along liberal lines, while democratic rule introduced where the state is autocratic tends to develop along populist lines. Liberal democracy is a viable form of government, while populist democracy readily gives way to new forms of autocracy. Where democracy emerges from some sort of *limited* minority rule, as in constitutional monarchism or classical (aristocratic) republicanism, it does not involve that sharp discontinuity in authority which marks the transition from the arbitrary rule of an autocrat to popular rule. That rapid transition from autocracy to democracy generally involves major discontinuities in authority is evident: in the form of transition itself, which characteristically is revolutionary; in the sponsorship of popular rule, which characteristically is an extremist mass movement; and in the tenure of democratic government, which tends to be short. The displacement of the *ancien régime* in France, followed by the triumph of the Jacobins and then the *coup d'état* of the 18th Brumaire, is the classic case in point. The introduction of popular rule in England led to no such fate, in part because it emerged from a limited monarchy and a constitutional tradition. In the one case the old ruling forms and groups were rent asunder by chiliastic mass movement, whereas in the other case the bases of authority were preserved by a process of accommodation between the old ruling groups and the rising classes.

Democratization along liberal lines requires a capacity on the part of ruling groups to accommodate new social elements, and progressively to share political rights and duties with them. Democratization along populist lines characteristically follows upon the failure of pre-existing governing groups to accommodate additional social elements, which thereupon seek the destruction of the old ruling groups and the institutional basis for their authority. De Tocqueville suggests that the decisive difference between England and France with respect to the introduction of democratic rule rested on the willingness of the English ruling groups to merge and mix with other groups versus the increasing unwillingness of the French ruling groups to do so.

From an early time a fundamental difference existed between the behavior of the governing classes in England and in France. The nobility, the cornerstone of medieval society, revealed in England a peculiar ability to merge and mix with other social groups, while in France it tended, on the contrary, to close its ranks and preserve its original purity of birth. In the earlier Middle Ages all Western Europe had a similar social system. But some time in the Middle Ages, one cannot say exactly when, a change pregnant with tremendous consequences occurred in the British Isles and in the British Isles only—the English nobility developed into an open aristocracy while the continental *noblesse* stubbornly remained within the rigid limits of a caste. (Quoted by Lippmann, 1956, p. 55)

Referring to these observations of De Tocqueville, Lippmann elaborates the argument as follows:

The crucial difference is between what we might call enfranchisement by assimilation into the governing class, as exemplified in England, and, *per contra,* enfranchisement by the overthrow and displacing of the governing class as exemplified in France. In the one the government remains but becomes more responsible and more responsive; in the other, the government is overthrown with the liquidation of the governing class. Although the two ways of evolution appear to have the same object—a society with free institutions under popular government—they are radically different and they arrive at radically different ends. The first way, that of assimilation, presumes the existence of a state which is already constitutional in principle, which is under laws that are no longer arbitrary, though they may be unjust and unequal. Into this constitutional state more and more people are admitted to the governing class and to the voting electorate. The unequal and the unjust laws are revised until eventually all the people have equal opportunities to enter the government and to be represented. Broadly speaking, this has been the working theory of the British movement towards a democratic society . . . and of the principal authors of the American Constitution, and this was how—though few of them welcomed it—they envisaged the enfranchisement of the whole adult population. The other way is that of the Jacobin revolution. The people rise to power by overthrowing the ruling class and by liquidating its privileges and prerogatives. This is the doctrine of democratic revolution which was developed by French thinkers in the eighteenth century and was put into practice by the Jacobin party in the French Revolution. (1956, pp. 55-6) [9]

In general the rapid introduction of democratic rule in a society that lacks a strong *constitutional* tradition leaves authority insecure and vulnerable to mass attacks. Where democracy arises outside of a constitutional system, it cannot draw upon the political past for legitimation, nor can it lean on previously nurtured habits of adherence to a rule of law. Therefore, it cannot summon the loyalty and understanding of either the old elites or the newly enfranchised classes, so that elements from both may join together in mass movements against the democratic regime. Fascist movements in Germany and Italy arose in part out of such a background. Consider the case of Italy, where the absence of a common, long-accepted constitutional tradition helped to retard the development of an adequate political consciousness and party system, and eventually led to the breakdown of the newly established and still infirm democracy. A study of the rise of fascism in Italy (Finer, 1935, pp. 64-7) lists a number of events in the Italian past which combined to deprive the Italian people of needed experience with constitutionalism. To begin with, Italy achieved its unification and independence relatively late. Divided into a host of petty states ruled by foreign governments, its population was consequently endowed with a spirit of resistance and hostility to government.

---

9. Cf. Bertrand de Jouvenel (1952, p. 282): "So it came about that the two countries [England and France] entered on the democratic era with very diverse dispositions. In one of them, the system of liberty, from being a right of persons of aristocratic origin, was to be progressively extended to all. . . . In France, on the other hand, the system of authority, the absolutist machine constructed by the Bourbon monarchy, was to fall into the hands of the people, taken in mass."

There was only limited experience with voting, for extension of the franchise was tardy, as compared with England, for example; but there was widespread experience with extra-legal mass actions, such as general strikes and uprisings, and government repression. Finally, there was also lacking a stable, established governing class which could impart legitimacy and competence to the new political system. In short, the situation was unfavorable for the orderly transition to popular rule. The failure of Italian democracy to sustain itself must in part be laid to its inhospitable political history.

A major difference between Italy and France (also Germany), on the one hand, and England and America, on the other, is one of marked versus mild discontinuities in political authority attendant upon the introduction of democratic rule. The transition from aristocratic to democratic rule in England has not involved sharp discontinuities because there already was a constitutional tradition to reduce the ground to be traversed between them. America experienced an even more continuous development, since it had no feudal past to break asunder (Hartz, 1955, p. 76). In De Tocqueville's words, "The great advantage of the American is that he has arrived at a state of democracy without having to endure a democratic revolution; and that he is born free without having to become so."[10]

The willingness of aristocracies to share authority with other social groups has not been the sole precondition for the development of a stable democratic order. The successful transition to popular government has also been based on the emergence of new social forces that *constrained* pre-existing ruling groups progressively to share their power and privileges with wider and wider sections of society. In particular, it has been based on the emergence of a plurality of independent groups jealously guarding their autonomy and authority. When society contains strong and independent

---

10. Quoted by Hartz (1955, frontispiece).

social forces, the optimum condition exists for combining authority and liberty. Multiple independent social groups support authority by sharing in it, that is, by themselves acting as intermediate authorities capable of ordering limited spheres of social life. In the absence of effectively self-governing groups, the state not only lacks restraint; it also lacks support. In eighteenth century France, for example, the centralization of power had gone so far that by 1789 "it had succeeded in eliminating all intermediate authorities," with the result that "nothing had been left that could obstruct the central government, but, by the same token, nothing could shore it up" (De Tocqueville, 1955, pp. 68, 137). The popular government created by the Revolution suffered a fate similar to that which befell the *ancien régime,* since it, too, was neither restrained nor protected in the absence of independent social organizations.[11]

A plurality of independent groups supports liberty at the same time that it supports authority. The sphere of liberty is enlarged when independent groups constrain one another, and the state, to seek an accommodation of interests in the form of certain rights—of free association, free expression, due process of law, and so forth. Thus, the English nobility demanded certain of these rights from the Crown in the first place to protect itself from the increasing power of the Crown; and subsequently elements of the gentry played a similar role toward both nobility and Crown.

A telling example of this historical development is provided by the nature and function of the House of Commons during the Late Middle Ages. Whereas in the continental system of estates the nobility and bourgeois were sharply distinguished, in the English Parliament the great nobility sat in the House of Lords, and the gentry sat "cheek by jowl" with the burghers in the House of Commons. This arrange-

---

11. In this respect, French revolutionary thought was self-defeating, in that it advocated the destruction of all independent social organization. See p. 139 below.

ment, which weakened the distinctions of feudalism, could develop in England more readily than on the continent because of the greater degree of intermarriage and communication between classes in England. Being so constituted, the Commons was able to play a major role in the development of liberal democracy, for it found political leverage as a "third party, holding the balance, and courted by the principals in the warfare of State." In the struggle between king and nobility, and among the nobles themselves, the House of Commons could advantageously act as umpire, a role it could the more easily play, since the mixed composition of the Commons meant "their interests were not wholly bound up with either Barons or King" (Trevelyan, 1953, pp. 261-3).

Another noteworthy aspect of the role of independent social groups in the development of firm social foundations for liberal democracy is to be found in the religious sphere. The rise of *religious nonconformity* was a major force making for the accommodation of diverse interests in the form of individual rights. Nonconformist groups not only nurtured the *idea* of individual rights (though often they did not do that) ; they were *training-grounds* and *organized bases* for the exercise of these rights. In particular, they were voluntary associations ready and able to fight for their right to exist. Thus, whereas France contained few independent groups to translate the ideal of the "rights of man and the citizen" into a living reality, England and later America overflowed with fiercely dissenting groups, jealously guarding their members from outside efforts to prevent the freedom of individual conscience, and the freedom to organize voluntarily in association of like-minded believers. "This principle of voluntary association was later translated from religion into politics, where it became the life principle of the free, democratic society" (Ebenstein, 1954, p. 165).[12] More than just the principle, the *habits* of free association

12. Cf. Lindsay (1943, p. 258).

were inculcated by religious dissent, first within the middle classes and subsequently within the working classes. Many an English working-class leader was formed in the nonconformist congregation.

It was in the village chapels of the 18th and 19th centuries that many local leaders of working-class organizations learned to think for themselves, as well as to conduct public meetings and administer finances. Wherever nonconformity was strong, labor unions and cooperatives were strong; in fact, the trade unions have been aptly called the present-day descendants of the earlier nonconformist congregations. (Ebenstein, 1954, p. 165)

In sum, closely associated with the rise of independent social classes, the emergence of independent religious groups helped to prepare the social foundations for liberal democracy in the Anglo-American world by promoting individual rights and by preparing people to exercise these rights.

If the strength of liberal democracy in England has been due in part to the emergence of strong and independent social classes, the failure of liberal democracy in Germany appears to be associated with the failure of its middle classes fully to develop a political style of their own. Whereas in England "the crown and aristocracy in the nineteenth century became assimilated in a middle-class ethos, the German middle classes were assimilated into the authoritarian and bureaucratic pattern of the Prussian monarchy." As a result, the German middle classes "failed to develop in any adequate sense a tradition of rational political discussion and of political participation, and the organizational and communications structure necessary to support such a tradition" (Almond, 1957, pp. 195-6).

This interpretation of the failure of the middle classes to support German democracy, in common with all theories which stress the importance of the middle classes for democracy, finds in the accommodation of independent social forces the best guarantee against the abuse of power. Such interpretations, therefore, could not judge mass society to be a secure base for democratic rule or individual freedom, since a mass society lacks strong independent social forces.

A contrary view stresses only the negative consequences of social pluralism for individual freedom. The individual, it is argued, must be freed from the shackles of privileged groups, such as the nobility, church, and corporation. This view, epitomized in French revolutionary and Marxist thought, finds in the mass society the social conditions required for thorough-going freedom, since in mass society all institutional sources of privilege are abolished in favor of the individual and the state (Nisbet, 1953, p. 118). French revolutionary thought propounded the thesis that the individual was to be freed from all social restraints:

All the existing traditions, established institutions, and social arrangements were to be overthrown and remade, with the sole purpose of securing to man the totality of his rights and freedoms, and liberating him from all dependence. . . . All the emphasis came to be placed on the destruction of inequalities, on bringing down the privileged to the level of common humanity, and on *sweeping away all intermediate centres of power and allegiance, whether social classes, regional communities, professional groups or corporations.* Nothing was left to stand between man and the State. (Talmon, 1952, pp. 249-50; italics added)

Marx shared this belief that the realization of freedom required the removal of all sources of inequality and therefore of conflict. He asserted that only by means of one final conflict between capitalists and workers could the free and harmonious order be achieved. In other words, the achievement of freedom requires a revolutionary break with all pre-existing forms of authority. The lower classes constitute the natural basis for a political movement bent on destroying all inequalities. In the case of Germany, for example, the Marxist view stresses the failure of working-class organizations, especially the Social Democracy, to act decisively to destroy the power and privileges of big business.[13] The liberal view, on the other hand, finds in the middle classes the

---

13. See, for example, F. Neumann (1944).

critical source of support for individual freedom, since the specific interests of the middle classes favor the proliferation of centers of power independent of the state. In the case of Germany, as we have noted, this view stresses the failure of the middle classes to develop independently of the state as a contributing cause to the defeat of freedom and democracy in that country.[14]

We may find a clue to the class base of liberal democracy in the position of those who want neither liberty nor democracy. The Nazis, for example, emphasize the role not of one class or another, but of the race—hence, in effect, of no class. For only by the abolition of all independent class formations can a thorough-going totalitarianism be realized. The Communists call for a classless society in the name of freedom, and proceed to destroy independent classes in order to create a totalitarian society wherever they come to power. Their inability to tolerate independent sources of power extends even—and perhaps especially—to organizations of the class in whose name the Communists seek power: working-class organizations, such as trade unions, have suffered the same fate under communism as all other forms of association. This suggests that individual freedom does not flourish when classes are destroyed, but that it depends on the mutual accommodation of the several classes. Furthermore, the genesis of liberal democracy depends not on the destruction of any class, nor on the abolition of conflict among classes, but on the progressive opening of the upper classes, and on the increased power and participation of the middle and lower classes. When the introduction of democratic rule is based on the continuous opening up of the class structure, then no major segment of the society will be alienated from it. When, on the other hand, democratic rule

---

14. See, for example, Almond (1957). We have already noted that the aristocratic view stresses the importance of the upper class in securing liberty, if not democracy. Thus each class finds its champion as the alleged basis of the free society.

is introduced by means of the sudden destruction of the old regime, then the new ruling groups cannot lean on pre-existing principles of legitimacy or on institutional procedures to stabilize their authority. As a result, they are vulnerable to sudden displacement by mass-oriented elites: the triumph of the Bolsheviks and the Nazis are the two most notable cases in point.

In summary, where the introduction of democratic rule is based on a pluralist society, especially a balance of classes and religious groups, it will tend to be strong and viable; but where its introduction is not accompanied by multiple independent groups capable of fighting for the sustenance of individual rights, and at the same time ready to support a basic framework of authority, democracy may readily lose out to new forms of autocracy.

Chapter 7

Discontinuities In Community

MARKED DISCONTINUITIES in authority provide the opportunity for totalitarian elites to seize power in the name of the masses, and thereby subvert democratic processes. Sharp discontinuities in community create the masses which totalitarian elites can utilize in their search for total power. The transformation of the rural-agrarian community into an urban-industrial community is fraught with peril in this respect, since at best this change involves pervasive disruption in the relations of large numbers of people. But many a society has come through this perilous period of transition without raising up new autocracies. Therefore, urbanization and industrialization need not necessarily summon mass tendencies which carry the day. On the contrary, they may be accompanied by new forms of association which decisively counter mass tendencies. We shall be concerned to show in this section that the rate and mode of urbanization and industrialization go far toward determining the extent to which the transformation of community is won at the price of creating masses available for mobilization by totalitarian movements. Although they are inextricably intertwined, we may consider urbanization and industrialization separately.

Urbanization

Many students of modern society have argued that urbanization generates masses. In fact, the conception of urban society held by many sociologists bears a close resemblance to the model of mass society as it is envisioned by the democratic critics. Those who conceive of the "urban way of life" in terms of secularization, individuation, and the like, imply that the modern city is the quintessence of mass society.[15]

If urbanization by itself were productive of masses, we would expect to find that the most highly urbanized societies exhibited the most mass characteristics. Yet it is highly questionable whether the more urbanized societies manifest the greater amount of political extremism; fascism triumphed in highly urbanized Germany, but also in much less urbanized Italy. Among Western countries since World War II, Communist parties have been strongest in France and Italy; and they have been weakest in Britain and the United States. Yet among these same countries, France and Italy rank low in degree of urbanization, while Britain and the United States rank high. More precisely, if 15 Western countries are ranked both according to the proportion of people who live in cities over 20,000 and according to the proportion of votes for the Communist party in 1953 (or the closest election to that year), the rank-order correlation is $-.61$.[16] Thus, there

---

15. See Simmel (1950); Park (1952); Wirth (1956, especially pp. 110-32); Tonnies (1940, especially pp. 261-75). The greater part of purely sociological (rather than political) analysis of mass society is represented by these works and those which are based upon them. The conception of mass society as the atomized society contained in these writings places the mainstream of sociological concern with mass society in the category of the "democratic criticism," as we delineated this perspective in Part I. For a critical assessment of these theories of urban life in light of recent research on patterns of participation in urban areas, see Greer (1958).

16. Urban data assembled from censuses of 1950, or the closest year thereto, by International Urban Research, University of California (Berkeley). For our purposes, countries were selected for computation of the correlation coefficient on the basis of availability of data on both urbanization and Communist vote. In addition to those already named, countries included are Australia, Austria, Belgium, Canada, Netherlands, Norway, Sweden, Switzerland, and West Germany.

is a negative relation between the extent to which societies are urbanized and the size of Communist support, *even though Communist parties get their major support from large cities within each country.*

In general, the proportion of a population supporting extremist movements like communism and fascism does not increase with the proportion living in cities, among Western countries. Certain *kinds* of extremist movements recruit disproportionately from urban segments *within* a country, however, while other kinds acquire a relatively greater share of their following from rural areas. Thus, the 1932 Nazi vote was found to correlate inversely with the size of city, the Communist vote directly, and the Socialist vote did not correlate (Pratt, 1938, chap. viii). Communist strength in cities has been observed in many countries; e.g., in Canada, Montreal, Toronto, and Winnipeg; in Denmark, Copenhagen; in England, London; in Finland, Helsinki, Turku, and Tampere; in France, Paris; in Holland, Amsterdam; in Russia in 1917, Moscow and Petrograd; in the United States, New York.[17]

The metropolis is the more congenial environment for communism as against fascism. The rural community, as the center of the forces of traditionalism, possesses a greater affinity for fascism than communism. Communism's basic values are associated with technology and equality, and therefore find a more ready response in the city. Fascism, on the other hand, in one of its faces, is a revolutionary expression of these traditional values which have been threatened by the development of the urban-industrial order, and therefore finds a greater response in rural areas.

There [in rural areas] insecurity has tended to be structured in terms of a felt threat to the traditionalized values. The typical reaction has been of an overdetermined "fundamentalist" type.

17. For data on Communist strength in these cities, see U. S. Department of State (1956, pp. 9, 19, 21); Radkey (1950, p. 34); Lipset and Linz (1956, chap. vii).

Aggression has turned toward symbols of the rationalizing and emancipated areas which are felt to be "subversive" of these values. (Parsons, 1942, p. 145)

These observations on rural-urban differences pertain to variations between *types* of mass movements. If we could compute the proportion of the population engaged in *all* kinds of mass movements, we would *not* expect it to be positively associated with the degree of urbanization among Western societies. What appears to be more important as a source of mass tendencies than the *degree* of urbanization is the *process* of urbanization, especially rapid rates of change in the size and composition of the population residing in an area. Where the process of urbanization has been going on for a long time, there is a greater opportunity for the emergence of new social forms to mediate between the individual and the "great society." The oft-noted proliferation of voluntary associations in the metropolis is the cardinal case in point. But where the process of urbanization is in its initial phases, social adaptations to conditions of city life are less likely to have been developed, and urban masses are more likely to result.

The *rapid* influx of large numbers of people into *newly* developing urban areas invites mass movements. A study of mass movements during the Late Middle Ages reports that these movements flourished in areas undergoing rapid urbanization, where industry and trade were developing and where the population was increasing rapidly (Cohn, 1957, pp. 21-32). It was among the newly urbanized masses rather than among the peasantry that revolutionary chiliasm ran strongest. For all of their poverty and hardships, the peasants had cohesive kinship and communal bonds sanctioned by tradition. They were relatively unavailable for the radical break with the social order entailed by the pursuit of millennial goals. This was true for those peasants who were rooted in the land. But for those who left the country for the cities springing up in Northwestern Europe during the later Middle Ages, no such network of social relations existed to provide support. Many lacked employment, and became beggars or roamed in gangs through the towns. Those who found unskilled work had no guild organization to protect them. And even skilled workers (for example, weavers) employed in industries which made goods for export could not rely on their guilds for protection against disruptions of trade.

These atomized urban masses were readily available for chiliastic movements which arose in Northwestern Europe during the Late Middle Ages:

Journeymen and unskilled workers, peasants without land or with too little land to support them, beggars and vagabonds, the unemployed and those threatened with unemployment, the many who for one reason or another could find no assured and recognized place—such people, living in a state of chronic frustration and anxiety, formed the most impulsive and unstable elements in medieval society. Any disturbing, frightening or exciting event—any kind of revolt or revolution, a summons to a crusade, an interregnum, a plague or a famine, anything in fact which disrupted the normal routine of social life—acted on these people with peculiar sharpness and called forth reactions of peculiar violence. . . . These were the people whose anxieties drove them to seek messianic leaders. (Cohn, 1957, pp. 29-30, 74)

The rapid influx of large numbers of people into a new organization (as well as a new area) provides opportunities for mass-oriented elites to penetrate the organization. This is particularly true during the formative periods of organization, for at such times external constraints must carry the burden of social control until the new participants have come to internalize the values of the organization. Communist groups have won major successes in labor organizations during periods of rapid growth, as in the formative period of the C.I.O. during the latter part of the 1930's. At this time, the new unions provided excellent opportunities, that were quickly seized by organizationally wise Communists, to rise to leadership positions. Although the Communists had hitherto failed to make much headway in the unions, they now achieved considerable influence in electrical, transport, mine, maritime, auto, and other unions (Howe and Widick, 1949, p. 149).

Revolutionaries (most prominently Communists) also gained control of the Paris labor organization and several national unions at a time when the French labor movement was swollen by a large influx of new workers who lacked prior experience in union life and who found no apparatus able to absorb them. This occurred following World War I, and then was repeated during the 1930's. In the latter period,

the Communist party, momentarily surprised and even annoyed by the swamping of the unions by the inrush of members, quickly threw itself into the work of organizing the new recruits and the swollen unions. . . . With the CGT's shortage of organizers and officials, Communist party activists moved into positions of leadership of this "new horde who knew nothing of traditional unionism." They were most effective in the Paris region, where the traditional unionism "was practically dissolved in a bath of sulphuric acid." By 1938 the Communists had moved from a minority position at reunification [of the CGT in 1935] into control of the national metal, chemical, food, agriculture, leather, electric power, and building trades unions. (Lorwin, 1954, p. 75)

The sudden and large influx of new population elements into a community often is perceived by the old residents as a threat to their status and control. They often respond to this threat by organizing anti-immigrant movements, which qualify as mass movements by virtue of their direct and unrestrained intervention in the life of the community. For example, Nativistic movements in America grew rapidly just after the peak of each major immigration wave: Native Americans in the 1840's, Know Nothings in the 1850's, Old Klan in the 1860's, American Protective Association in the 1890's, New Klan in the 1920's.[18] The Klan was successful during the 1920's primarily because the Catholic immigration up to World War I became a highly visible target

---

18. See Micklen (1924, pp. 162-6) and Loucks (1936, pp. 4-16).

for the frustration attendant upon severe competition for jobs during the post-war depression. (The fact that the Klan collapsed quickly in the later twenties may be attributed not so much to the integration of Catholic immigrants into urban life as to the anti-immigration law of 1924, the end of the depression and the resulting diminution in competition for jobs in 1925, and the revelation of criminal behavior of certain Klan leaders.) [19]

The rapid ascendancy of urban centers also tends to be perceived by older (rural) population elements as a threat to their status and control. The links between rural communities and the larger society tend to disintegrate during periods of urbanization, as in the decline of the rural church, newspaper, political representative, and other intermediate relations. This lack of intermediate relations on the part of rural people is evident in certain backward areas of countries dominated by large urban centers. Out of such areas have sprung some of the most extreme mass movements of modern times, reactions against the loss of opportunities for participation, status, and power resulting from the rise of new areas and symbols of dominance. These expressions of hostility and resentment on the part of those who feel themselves by-passed in the process of urbanization play a major role in the politics of many countries. As such, they point up the importance of not confounding mass movements with class movements. Mass movements have mobilized alienated rural populations as well as atomized urban populations. The rise of Poujadism in rural France illustrates this.

The Poujadist movement is based on those areas in France which have been undergoing rapid depopulation. Out of eleven solidly Poujadist departments, nine have lost population. Not only has this mass movement found its major popular support in areas undergoing depopulation, but further, in the declining regions, it is the rural population

---

19. See Loucks (1936, pp. 164-95).

which has sustained the most marked losses. Census data for 1954 show that in departments which are losing population, the cities have either gained population or are losing less heavily than the department as a whole. And it is particularly in the country and in the small towns that the Poujade movement has obtained its greatest successes. It has had much more difficulty in penetrating the cities (Hoffmann, 1956, pp. 12-13).

There is a fundamental connection between the Poujadist success in rural areas undergoing depopulation and its attraction for the old middle class of small businessmen and artisans. For it is precisely in these declining areas that the number of businesses is very high and their income very low. These are the areas of France that are not participating in the increasing modernization and prosperity of the industrial north.

The starting point and stronghold of Poujadism is in [this] "underdeveloped" southeast France. . . . Here the discontented of all parties, including a considerable number of Communists . . . went over to Poujade as the loudest and most active malcontent. . . . The 2,600,000 votes his movement got in the [1956] elections came from all sectors of that disoriented mass of floating voters whose convulsive changes of mind are one sure symptom of the French political malaise. . . . [This] movement of small tradesmen, loud-mouths, and illiterates, this "uprising of the unpoliticals" . . . is nourished by the same instinctive popular reaction against the customs and usages of French parliamentarism which gave De Gaulle his following. (Luethy, 1956, p. 304)

The Poujade movement illustrates the thesis that population changes may have mass-producing consequences when they reflect and accentuate the isolation of those areas from which people are moving. The very uneven development of the two parts of France breeds mass tendencies in that part which is being depopulated, even as it also favors similar tendencies in that part which is undergoing rapid urbanization. Since rapid urbanization characteristically accompanies rapid industrialization, examination of the mass-producing consequences of the growth of industry will also shed further light on the relation between urbanization and mass behavior.

Industrialization

Another process related to the genesis of mass relations and mass movements is industrialization. Here, again, it has been commonly assumed that industrialization per se generates mass movements. But as in the case of urbanization, political extremism is not positively associated with degree of industrialization among countries which already have a good amount of industry. When fifteen Western countries are ranked according to the proportion of the male labor force in nonagricultural occupations and proportion of votes for the Communist party in 1953 (or the closest election to that date), the rank-order correlation is —.76.[20] Thus, there is a strong negative relation between the extent to which societies are industrialized and the strength of communism within the Western world, *even though Communist parties get more support from workers in large (versus small) industrial plants within each country*.[21] Industrialization is mass-producing not in the *degree* to which industry has displaced agriculture, but insofar as the *manner* in which industry is introduced involves marked *discontinuities* in social organization.

Greater discontinuities tend to occur in the *early* period of industrialization, and that is the time when mass move-

---

20. Labor force data compiled by International Urban Research, University of California (Berkeley), from the United Nations *Demographic Yearbook, 1956*, Table 12. Using per capita commercial energy expenditure as an index of industrialization, the correlation with size of the Communist vote is —.83. Data on energy expenditure compiled by International Urban Research from the United Nations *Statistical Yearbook, 1956*, Table 127.

21. The relation between size of industrial plant and Communist vote is reported in Lipset *et al.* (1954, pp. 1139, 1141).

ments flourish. The mitigation of mass tendencies depends on the creation of new social forms, especially trade unions, to mediate between the industrial labor force and the national society. This takes time, as is apparent in any comparison between new and old industrial communities. The latter typically have evolved not only trade unions, but they have nurtured types of men who have internalized the industrial discipline, as well as expectations commensurate with the objective possibilities of satisfaction and achievement in an industrial system. New industrial communities, on the other hand, generally have not had the time to make such adaptations.

Consequently, industrialization initially is more likely to increase the rate and size of mass movements, especially as it tends to create an "internal proletariat"; but subsequently it may decrease mass tendencies in favor of more moderate social movements, especially when the higher classes allow for a more or less rapid reincorporation of workers into the society (Bendix, 1956, pp. 434-7). In addition, where industrial development proceeds at a very *uneven* rate, and creates highly visible differentials in economic gains, strong feelings of alienation from the existing order tend to appear among those in the less rapidly developing sectors and areas. Since it is with highly advanced industrialization that economic differentials among areas and classes tend to decline significantly, the less advanced of the industrial countries, such as Italy, manifest the greater economic disparities. Thus the Italian Communists have enrolled large numbers of industrial workers, *particularly in the less modernized plants* (Einaudi *et al.*, 1951, pp. 43-4) :

Plants, in order of increasing modernization	Communist party members
Ansaldo (facing complete bankruptcy)	85%
Ilva (beginning modernization)	77
Fiat (more modernized than Ilva)	70
Olivetti (renovation far along)	66
Rossi (highly profitable textiles)	58

Of course, it should not be inferred that modernization per se is sufficient to overcome political alienation.

Alienation resulting from industrialization cannot be mitigated unless the movement into industry is a continuous one, thereby providing "old hands" with established expectations to socialize new workers, as well as a progressive one, thereby providing greater achievements over time. The critical period usually is the initial one, both for the society as a whole and for particular individuals entering the industrial labor force. The more rapid the initial industrialization, the greater the alienation. Furthermore, the greater the social disparity between pre-industrial and industrial conditions of a newly recruited labor force, the more likely it is to engage in extremist mass action.

Russia, during the first part of this century, witnessed the very rapid growth of an industrial labor force for whom the ways of the factory and the city were totally alien. Beginning in the 1890's, Russia was undergoing a very rapid industrialization, in which peasants were recruited into factories directly from the communal life of the *mir*. Unlike the development of industry in countries which industrialized over a considerable period of time—progressing from handicrafts to small factories, and thence to large ones—industry in Russia was introduced very rapidly in the form of the large factory.[22] The fact that these factories generally were very large, and located in big cities, made the peasant's transition from village life to urban-industrial conditions much more difficult, and hindered his integration into the workplace (Brutzkus, 1953, p. 537). One result was a very rapid turnover of industrial labor; a report on the factories in Petersburg for 1904 indicated that "the whole work force had to be replaced about once a year" (Bendix, 1956, p. 177). A second result was the opportunity for revolutionaries to

---

22. According to Trotsky (1932, p. 10), enterprises involving more than 1000 workers employed only 17.9% of the workers in the United States in 1914, as compared with 41.4% in Russia (57.3% in the Moscow district).

carry on agitational activities among the highly atomized working class. Workers did not have alternative ways of seeking amelioration of their plight, for freedom to organize was withheld. Denied any legal means of improving their position, "the only remaining alternative for young and audacious members of the working class was to engage in revolutionary activities" (Brutzkus, 1953, p. 538). Since the Bolsheviks were the only revolutionary group to concentrate their agitation among industrial workers, and since these workers were concentrated in Moscow and Petrograd, these cities became the great strongholds of the Bolsheviks in 1917, their lesser strength being in the small industrial towns, and their least support in the villages (Radkey, 1950, p. 38).

Norway was the only Scandinavian country which saw its labor party join the Third International following the Russian Revolution.[23] (The Norwegian labor movement subsequently quit the Comintern, and became firmly attached to democratic institutions.) Between 1907 and 1917, Norway had undergone rapid industrial expansion as a result of the development of hydro-electric power. Its labor force was recruited from smallholders without previous experience in steady employment whereas many workers in Sweden and Denmark were recruited from skilled craftsmen who brought with them experience in guild and shop. Furthermore, living and working conditions were very poor in Norway, somewhat better in Sweden, and appreciably better in Denmark. It was this uprooted industrial labor force, living in boom towns, that came to constitute the mass base of the extremist Norwegian labor movement.

In contrast to Norway, Denmark experienced more gradual industrialization; and the labor movement of this country followed more moderate paths. The Swedish labor movement exhibited greater extremist tendencies than the Danish movement (although not so extreme as Norway) prior to

23. The following discussion of the Scandinavian labor movements is based on Galenson (1952, pp. 147-55).

World War I. Again, this difference corresponds to the speed and mode of industrialization in the two countries. In Denmark, the tempo was more gradual and smaller factories were involved, with emphasis on highly skilled labor. In Sweden, the process was more rapid and factories larger. The skilled workers with previous experience in factories and guilds tended to take the leadership of the new Danish industrial labor force, while socialist intellectuals and unskilled workers played a greater role in Sweden.

Thus it was that an extremist movement arose within the Swedish trade unions and Social Democratic party to oppose the moderate democratic policies which prevailed prior to the rapid expansion of industries. At the same time, a strong anarcho-syndicalist movement emerged in those industries which were expanding rapidly.

However, in Denmark the prior development of multiple working-class organizations prepared the social foundations for democratic action. For example, 80 per cent of the 65 trade unions formed in Copenhagen between 1870 and 1880 were in occupations in which a guild monopoly had existed. The most stable and moderate unions were preceded by strong guilds. This continuity in working-class organization paved the way for a democratically-oriented labor movement in this country. The marked discontinuities in Swedish and Norwegian working-class organization appear to be related to the greater degree of extra-legal mass action of their early labor movements. Without strong organizations of their own, out of which a genuine class leadership can emerge, workers tend to turn to radical intellectuals and other outside leadership. In addition, workers lack those day to day achievements of strong trade unions that legitimize moderate and pragmatic aims. In short, when workers engage in political action without prior formation of their own organizations and their own leadership to guide and mediate that action, it will tend to take on a mass character.

Distrust of parliamentary government, and support for

anarchist, syndicalist, and Communist actions against the state has characterized workers in France, Italy, and Spain. In each case, trade unions often were either suppressed or granted only *de facto* recognition by business and government.[24]

France has witnessed a long history of business and governmental attempts to destroy trade unions, or at least to prevent them from gaining a legitimate place in the industrial order. Many business leaders not only violated collective bargaining agreements, but they often blocked the administration of reform legislation designed to improve wages and working conditions. Right-wing governments used the power of the state, especially the right of conscription, to break strikes. As recently as 1939-40, business and government used the opportunity of the war to weaken the position of organized labor. The subsequent Vichy regime went further in its attempt to destroy labor's power and rights. Such actions have discouraged French workers from seeking an accommodation of their interests within the existing system, and they have discouraged the emergence of moderate labor leaders who did not desire the destruction of the existing order. However, moderate leadership did emerge in those industries where labor was less threatened and more secure. Thus, workers who backed the moderate socialists rather than the Communists before World War II tended to be among the better organized: their stable and powerful unions gave these workers a place in the existing order. The growth and persistence of Communist strength, on the other hand, is closely related to the availability of French workers who have felt like outsiders in a society in which business and government frequently have refused to recognize the legitimacy of their organizations, leaders, and demands (Einaudi *et al.*, 1951, pp. 6-9).[25]

Italian and Spanish workers have had somewhat similar

---

24. The following discussion is indebted to Lipset and Linz (1956).
25. See also Saposs (1954, p. 309).

experiences. As in France, the business classes continually resisted trade union efforts to secure a legitimate position in society. Even more than in France, Fascist movements have successfully suppressed working-class organizations and leaders. And just as in France, these organizations and leaders have responded by supporting extremist doctrines. In Spain, moderate socialism always was weak, while anarchism and later communism were relatively strong prior to the Franco regime. In Italy, anarchism was comparatively strong before the Fascist coup, and communism (including the closely allied Nenni Socialists) has had a much larger following than moderate socialism since the demise of Mussolini.

In conclusion, it is no accident that communism followed anarcho-syndicalism, among large numbers of workers in France, Italy, and Spain. Anarcho-syndicalism, with its refusal to recognize the reality of politics and its disdain for parliamentary democracy, prevented an effective working relationship of the unions with the socialist parties, to the great mischief of both, and helped leave workers poorly prepared later to distinguish between democratic political protest and Communist politics (Lorwin, 1958, pp. 345-6).

In Argentina, freshly industrialized and urbanized workers were readily mobilized by the Peronista, a Fascist-like mass movement. Specifically, the rapid industrialization beginning in the 1930's uprooted large numbers of rural people and transformed them into factory workers without any prior preparation or experience. The problem of integration of the workers was aggravated by the growing urban concentration about Greater Buenos Aires. The rate and manner of industrialization and urbanization resulted in a working class without prior experience in labor organization or political activity. The suppression of labor unions and political activities for more than a decade increased the availability of workers for mass movements (Germani, 1956).[26]

---

26. Cf. pp. 146-7 above.

Thus, industrialization and urbanization are mass-producing to the extent that they involve sharp discontinuities in community, that is, to the extent that they produce rootlessness. In this connection, a study of Swedish communism reports that, in a number of cases, "social isolation, and hence communism, tend to develop when large numbers of people are uprooted from their homes and find employment elsewhere." In light of these cases, this study suggests that communism is the "religion of the rootless." But we are reminded that "rootlessness is not necessarily a concomitant only of industrialization." Thus, in the district in Sweden that is most strongly Communist, farming and forestry are the major occupations, and there is no industry at all (Davison, 1954-55, pp. 378, 383-4).

Although it is undoubtedly true that there are other sources of mass tendencies, the very rapid expansion of cities and industries has constituted perhaps the most general source of social atomization in the modern world, insofar as they have inhibited the growth of new forms of group life to replace the village community, extended family, and guild which they destroyed.[27] More concretely, industrialization, when it is not accompanied by the evolution and legitimation of trade unions, whether as a result of the weakness of pre-industrial workingmen's associations (as in Norway), or as a result of the suppression of labor unions (as in France, Italy, Russia, and Spain), favors the atomization of the working class and the formation of mass movements.

In summary, as in the instance of urbanization, there probably is not a positive relation, in industrial societies, between the proportion of the labor force employed in industry and the proportion of the population engaged in mass movements. Specifically with respect to the strength of demo-

---

27. This is clearly indicated by the success of the Anabaptists among the unorganized mass of workers created by the rapid growth of the cloth industry in sixteenth century Holland. In particular, the new form of industry undermined the guilds (Cohn, 1957, p. 281).

cratic habits in a society, the more industrialized countries appear to be the stronger democracies (Germany is an exception). Extremist mass movements are characteristic of the early period of rapid industrialization, for that is the time in which the most severe discontinuities in community life occur. To the extent that large parts of Asia and Africa are just now moving into the initial period of industrialization, these countries may expect to witness a plethora of mass movements, depending in part on the rate and mode of industrialization.

Chapter 8

Discontinuities
in Society

MARKED DISCONTINUITIES in authority and community produce long-run mass tendencies. Sudden tears in the fabric of a whole society tend to precipitate short-run mass tendencies. (This, of course, is a difference in degree; factors that generate a chronic state of the masses may be operating along with those associated with a transitory mass condition.) Such crises often follow upon severe depression or national defeat, and simultaneously tend to weaken both community and authority. As a consequence, they favor the rise of mass movements. Crises are especially likely to have this effect in a society marked by a chronic mass condition. In this sense, they test society, revealing its underlying strengths and weaknesses.

Depression

Societies which are very poor do not experience marked discontinuities in life-conditions, as compared with wealthier societies. A *steady* level of poverty favors the stabilization of social and cultural relations. But if economic conditions are changing, then people are more likely to feel frustrated and insecure as they compare their lot with the one that has been held out to them as their legitimate condition, and with other classes and countries that enjoy a higher standard of living. Hence, countries undergoing economic growth, rather than economically stagnant ones, manifest the greater discontent when discontinuities in economic conditions occur.

Among countries that have already experienced considerable industrial development, those that have made the greater progress in raising the standard of living for the bulk of the population have produced the stronger democracies, whereas those countries that have experienced less progress possess the greater anti-democratic tendencies. One small but definite indication of this is provided by the relationship between per capita income in 1949 and per cent of the vote which went to the Communists in the first election held after that date, in 16 Western democracies.[28] *The rank-order correlation between per capita income and Communist vote is —.93.* At the same time, the correlation of per capita income with the socialist vote in these countries is only —.20, so that we are not measuring merely a leftward tendency in the less wealthy countries, but a revolutionary tendency against the existing democratic system.

Within industrial societies, sudden economic reversals do not always generate extremist responses. For example, in *three out of nine* European countries which held elections just before and after the Great Depression, the *Communist vote declined between 1928 and 1932.* However, if the *severity* of the depression is taken into account, changes in extremist voting fall into a pattern. Using the per cent of the labor force unemployed at the time of the first election following the onslaught of the depression as an indicator of the severity of the economic crisis,[29] and the per cent change in

28. Income statistics are from the United Nations Statistical Office, *Statistical Papers, Series E, No. 1* (1950, pp. 14-16).

29. Unemployment statistics are from the United Nations Statistical Office, *Statistical Yearbook, 1948* (pp. 84-5) and *Statistical Yearbook, 1955* (pp. 77-8); and Galenson and Zellner (1957).

the Communist vote over the last pre-depression election as an indicator of the extremist response to the crisis,[30] the correlation for these nine European countries is +.85. If the Fascist vote is included along with that of the Communist vote (excluding those countries which had no Fascist parties), the correlation increases to +.93. This suggests that *the more severe the crisis the greater the extremist response.* This is particularly important in light of the above observation to the effect that the extremist vote declined in three countries. Therefore, it cannot be the mere fact of crisis which calls forth mass movements, since all countries underwent the depression, yet some showed declining political extremism. Rather, it must be the intensity of crisis that is significant, for some countries suffered more severely from the depression's effects, and those countries showed the greatest percentage increase in political extremism.

When the crisis is relatively less severe, the electorate is more inclined to support pragmatic programs of amelioration within the established order. The orientation is less one of destruction and more one of improvement. Thus, there is a *negative* correlation of —.53 between the extent of unemployment and the percentage increase in the size of the democratic socialist vote in nine European countries between 1928 and 1932. Here, again, it may be observed that the crisis was associated with an absolute increase in the socialist vote in some countries, and with an absolute decrease in other countries. It was in those countries where the crisis was less severe that the democratic socialists were more likely to increase their strength. In all cases a sizable if minority party, the socialists had roots in the going system. Their members and supporters were more likely to continue to sustain their commitment to reform within the

---

30. We use per cent *change* in Communist vote, rather than per cent Communist vote, because we wish to rank countries by the relative *growth* of anti-democratic activity. Direct comparisons of Communist vote for several countries during the depression would be misleading because so much depends on the prior strength of the Communist party in each country.

system when their own social and psychological ties were not impaired beyond hope. In countries where existing social arrangements were so disrupted that they did not appear to offer any room for personal improvement in the future, the socialists and other moderates tended to lose votes to the Communists and other extremists.

Thus, unemployed German wage-workers went Communist in comparison with employed wage-workers, who stayed Socialist; and unemployed German white-collar workers went Nazi in comparison with employed white-collar workers, who stayed conservative or moderate (Pratt, 1936, chap. viii). The Nazis also found support in the working class, from among the "permanently unemployed who had given up hope of ever again finding work in the 'normal' way" (Anderson, 1945, p. 137). And they further gained a middle-class following from the dispossessed small businessmen, along with the unemployed salaried workers. The severe inflation wiped out the businessmen's savings, and the subsequent depression took away their incomes. The resulting widespread and deep economic insecurity destroyed the lower-middle-class faith in the prevailing social order, and made for high vulnerability to Nazi appeals (Schweitzer, 1955). The German peasants were the first to feel the depression; and they were hit particularly hard by it because they had been on top during and after World War I, so that they lost faster (if not more) than the other classes. The Nazis exploited this discontent first and more effectively than other parties (Heiden, 1944, pp. 334-5).[31] A leading Nazi agricultural expert went so far as to state: "The Third Reich will be a peasant Reich or it will not be at all."[32]

Such observations as these readily lend themselves to a simple economic interpretation of the rise of extremist movements. According to this interpretation, unemployed people seek out the movement promising the quickest and fullest

31. Cf. Bullock (1952, p. 139).
32. Quoted by Schweitzer (1955, p. 589).

improvement of their economic interests. This undoubtedly is part of the explanation of the relation between severity of depression and increase in Fascist and Communist vote. But economic analysis fails to account for the large number of people who engage in mass action against the democratic order when there is no economic crisis. Mass analysis, on the other hand, attempts to identify some of the general factors at work in all cases where widespread extremist mass movements develop, as in the early phase of industrialization, during periods of rapid population changes, in times of severe military defeat, as well as during acute and prolonged economic crises. Frustration of economic interests is hardly such a general factor. Nor is it likely by itself to create a psychology of the masses, namely, widespread alienation and suggestibility which prepares people psychologically for all kinds of extreme behavior they would reject as members of established groups and social institutions. Mass movements are not looking for pragmatic solutions to economic or any other kind of problem. If they were so oriented, their emotional fervor and chiliastic zeal, even the readiness for self-sacrifice by many of their members, would not characterize the psychological tone of these movements. In order to account for this tone, we must look beyond economic interests to more deep-seated psychological tendencies, and their social sources. In Part III of this study, we shall see to what extent Fascist and Communist movements are based on particular classes. In this section, we are concerned to show how unemployment creates psychological tendencies which prepare people for participation in Fascist and Communist movements.

Prolonged unemployment prepares people for mass movements by making multiple social ties inoperative. Studies of the unemployed in several countries demonstrate the critical nature of the job as a source of socially and psychologically integrating experience. The lack of a continuous occupation, more than any other circumstance, isolates the individual from his society. It does so in the first place by denying the individual the major basis of his self-respect in a culture which judges a man mainly by his occupation.[33] Interviews with unemployed skilled workers and white-collar employees in the New York area in 1935-36 revealed that a powerful sense of humiliation was associated with the inability to find employment.

> The general impression that the interviews make is that in addition to sheer economic anxiety the man suffers from deep humiliation. . . . [One] confessed that he lost his self-respect because of his unemployment. . . . Furthermore, for most of the men in our culture, work is apparently the sole organizing principle and the only means of self-expression. . . . [Without it,] they faced complete emptiness. (Komarovsky, 1940, pp. 74, 79, 81)

Unemployment has a debilitating effect, in the second place, because it undermines social relations and involvement in society. Denial of access to the occupational world directly cuts off a major source of interest in and understanding of one's environment. Indirectly it also tends to disrupt non-occupational relations, as the unemployed worker withdraws from contact with his fellows, sometimes even his family, in order to mitigate the shame he feels in their presence, or sometimes simply because the anxiety over meeting basic physical needs becomes all-consuming. Komarovsky (1940, p. 122) observed the extreme social isolation of the unemployed man and his family in New York during the depression: "The typical family in our group does not attend church, does not belong to clubs, and for months at a time does not have social contacts with anyone outside the family."

Further evidence of the withdrawal of the unemployed from both formal and informal social relations is provided by a study of unemployed workers in New Haven (see Table 9).

---

33. See Komarovsky (1940, pp. 74-5); Zawadski and Lazarsfeld (1935, pp. 238-40); and Eisenberg and Lazarsfeld (1938).

TABLE 9.—Proportion of 200 Unemployed Families Participating in Various Kinds of Activity Before and During Unemployment.

PER CENT WHO PARTICIPATED IN	Before Unemployment	During Unemployment
Trade unions	32	15
Clubs and lodges	60	31
Visits with relatives and friends	66	29
Chatting and gossiping randomly	0	12
Sitting around home	13	25

SOURCE: Bakke (1940, p. 14).

Under these conditions the unemployed worker loses touch with his society.

The reality of citizenship has been reduced by the loss of contact with organizations which participate to some extent in the larger interests of the community. The formal clubs, lodges, and trade unions through whose programs and affairs a man learns something of the larger issues in the community and gets a training in democracy—all these have been curtailed. Moreover the excursions which at least bring the worker in contact with a larger world than his own neighborhood have been severely cut down. . . . He spends more time at home, and frequently the newspaper has been stopped and the radio sold, so that even this source of contact with the larger world is reduced. (Bakke, 1940, pp. 16-7)

In short, prolonged unemployment operates as a severe depressant on the individual's relations to his society and himself. This would appear to be particularly true for those who lacked strong social ties prior to the depression (Komarovsky, 1940, p. 129). But it also holds, if to a lesser extent, for workers with a long history of collective activity and social solidarity; for example, a study of unemployed Polish workers disclosed their "disassociation of feelings of solidarity . . . [leaving] only scattered, loose, perplexed and hopeless individuals" (Zawadski and Lazarsfeld, 1935, p. 245).

In what sense are people in this condition of isolation available for mass action? The loss of binding relations to the established order enhances susceptibility to attacks on it. On the other hand, their very isolation makes it more difficult for extremist appeals to reach the unemployed; and, in addition, the unemployed may become apathetic rather than activistic. Therefore, unemployment is by no means always linked to mass behavior:

The experiences of unemployment are a preliminary step for the revolutionary mood but . . . they do not lead by themselves to a readiness for mass action. . . . [They] only fertilize the ground for revolution. (Zawadski and Lazarsfeld, 1935, p. 249)

Thus it is that unemployment sometimes calls forth extremist collective reactions, and at other times may be associated with political moderation or apathy. In the American studies of the unemployed, collective responses varied. For example, comparatively few of the unemployed in New Haven turned to direct action, although numerous promotional activities on the part of Communists and other radical groups provided opportunities for such action (Bakke, 1940, p. 69). For most of these men, resentment against the established institutions was not sufficient to overcome a traditional suspicion of collective or radical solution to their problems. In Chicago, however, there was found to be a close relation between increasing unemployment and such indicators of extremist activity as the number and circulation of Communist periodicals, the number of organizations affiliated or cooperating with the Communist party, the number of meetings sponsored by the Communist party and its affiliates, membership in the Communist party, and attendance at Communist demonstrations (Lasswell and Blumenstock, 1939, pp. 62, 64, 75, 81, 220-1, 232, 234, 366-8).

Granted that many unemployed people withdraw from all activity, nevertheless a larger proportion of unemployed than of employed workers flock to mass movements during depressions. Part of the appeal of these movements to the unemployed is based on their *activism:* they give people something to do, and this helps to overcome feelings of helplessness and uselessness. Totalitarian parties in particular provide their members with continuous activity, something not provided by the democratic parties. The activism of totalitarian parties is indicated by the higher level of activity of supporters of the Communist party compared with that of other political parties in France (Table 10).

TABLE 10.—Political Activity of Supporters of French Parties.

PER CENT WHO	SUPPORTERS OF					
	Communists	Socialists	MRP	Radicals	Conservatives	RPF
Sold papers, etc.	31	8	8	7	5	7
Sought support for party	51	32	35	28	29	42
Gave money	55	32	23	20	17	15

SOURCE: Williams (1954, p. 447).

In summary, extreme mass movements appeal to the unemployed on psychological as well as economic grounds, as ways of overcoming feelings of anxiety and futility, and of finding new solidarity and forms of activity.

Finally, unemployment which is widespread, prolonged, and severe engenders mass movements because it weakens the social foundation of elites as well as non-elites. The failure to cope with the crisis on the part of the governing groups increases self-doubt within these circles, as well as popular discontent with them. Consequently, the inability to terminate such crises, or, at least, to mitigate them, makes political and economic rulers highly vulnerable to direct pressure, such as unemployment demonstrations, marches on legislatures, and political violence in the streets. It also increases the readiness of individual members of elites to go over to the side of mass movements. In general, the demoralization of elites due to their ineffectiveness in coping with critical situations invariably appears to precede and summon mass actions against the social order. This may be observed in times of military defeat.

War

Severe war crises, as well as economic crises, summon mass tendencies, for they also suddenly jolt people out of their social niches and leave them defenseless against real or imagined dangers. Paramount among these dangers is military defeat, for then the state as well as the smaller social structures disintegrates. Threatened military defeat may strengthen rather than destroy the collective will to resist, but this in itself may be a form of mass mobilization. That the German defeat in the First World War prepared the way for an extraordinary (mass) mobilization is evidenced by the large number of political murders after the armistice and by the large number of self-constituted paramilitary bands that persisted long after "demobilization," to become the shock-troops of the Nazi movement in the succeeding years (S. Neumann, 1942, p. 109). In general, war crises of great severity clearly are mass-producing in their devastation of the very physical bases of both elite and non-elite.

The loss of legitimacy of an elite that presides over a major military defeat, along with its loss of control over the means of coercion, tends to produce an open power situation. Costly and exhausting military effort in World War I overstrained the social structure in Germany, Italy, and Russia, and culminated in the overthrow of the democratic regimes in these countries. The defeat in Germany was sudden and unexpected, thereby much more sharply damaging the sense of national integrity (Bullock, 1952, p. 51). The Versailles Treaty added to the national humiliation (Friedrich, 1954, p. 34). Even though on the victorious side, Italy was treated as a second-class power by the Allies; the resulting national humiliation here, too, undermined the legitimacy of the government. In both countries, the democratic regime lost control over the means of coercion. Weimar could not mobilize either the will or the capacity to suppress Nazi activity, even though it obviously was extra-legal in character, and involved numerous political murders. Nor could the majority moderates in the Italian parliament resist the widespread violence of the Squadristi armed by the military. In Italy, too, it is estimated that during 1921 and 1922 the Fascists were probably responsible for more than a thousand killings (Ebenstein, 1939, p. 28).[34] The inability of Tsardom and then the Provisional Government to effectively fight World War I caused the consequent great loss in national integrity and security in Russia. The revelation of impotence, incompetence, and degeneration in the highest circles damaged integrity; and losses in men, territory, and resources undermined security.[35] This snapped traditional ties to authority and boosted the Bolsheviks as the only ones openly proclaiming for peace at any price (Sumner, 1939, p. 113).[36] Furthermore, as in Germany and Italy, the Provisional Government could not conveniently suppress Bolshevik propaganda and organization.

In general, regimes are not overthrown by revolutions unless and until they have lost the loyalty of the armed forces or lost the will to use them effectively. Moderate, democratic regimes in particular may find it difficult to use force effectively against an extremist opposition (Brinton, 1952, pp. 94-104). Especially revealing in this respect have been socialist attitudes toward the use of force. When they have been in power and did not accept the use of force as a last resort to prevent conspiracies against the state, socialist regimes have been defeated by totalitarian movements. The

34. Cf. Borgese (1937, p. 226) and Salvemini (1927, pp. 56-7).
35. See Fainsod (1953, p. 85); Chamberlin (1935, p. 1); and Spargo (1919, pp. 85-6).
36. Cf. Kennan (1954, p. 26): "Totalitarianism came in the wake of a terribly costly and exhausting military effort, namely World War I, which in each case overshadowed the existing structure of society and culminated in the overthrow of the monarchical system and decisive disruption of the aristocracy." See also Florinsky (1931, p. 263).

failure to employ legal force against illegal force is illustrated by Socialist impotence in the face of the Bolshevik attack on the Provisional Government in Russia, and in the face of the combined Communist and Nazi attack on the Weimar Republic in Germany. (Socialists at times have not been so recalcitrant about using force when they have been out of power, and therefore in opposition to ruling groups. For example, Italian Socialists following World War I equivocated when it came to the question of employing violent methods.) [37]

Foreign occupation often counteracts mass tendencies that accompany lost wars, by closing off access to media of communication and the means of power, and by direct suppression of mass movements. In such countries as Germany, Italy, and Russia following World War I, the absence of foreign control permitted totalitarian elites to mobilize masses and overthrow existing regimes, whereas the occupation of Germany and Italy following World War II probably prevented the quick emergence of major mass movements.

Extreme discontinuities following upon total military defeat may be expected to produce atomization of relations on *all* levels of society. This appears to have happened in Germany following World War II. Not only did the defeat of Hitler wipe out the Nazi elite; it also led to the breakdown of the traditional bases of German elites, namely the military and civil service. The post-war period has witnessed the ascendancy of business elites in West Germany. By virtue of the great expansion of business and the newness of its ascendancy, the change in composition of elites from

37. Ebenstein (1939, p. 10) refers to the Italian Socialist party's "lack of decision as to the use of violence. Condemning its use against Socialists, the party approved its employment—at least in theory—against capitalism. Especially in Italy which, like Spain, looks back on a long tradition of Anarchism and Revolutionary Syndicalism, the Socialist party should have been more vigorous in its attitude towards violence as a political method. The failure to draw a clear line between itself and Revolutionary Syndicalism as to the mode of revolutionary action was to prove fatal to its very existence."

pre-Hitler to post-Hitler West Germany has involved the atomization of elites.

At the same time that the destruction of the Third Reich engendered atomization of elites in West Germany, it also has produced widespread privatization among the youth.

Whether questions addressed to [German labor youth] pertain to their own social and economic role or to some institutional pattern, [there are] few competent answers. They are not quite sure about the need for and the function of political parties. [In a Hamburg sample, 40% of the male youth thought one party would be enough, and 44% had no answer to the question of why one joins a political party.] There is a strong minority who feel that, rather than show interest in and responsibility for the politics of their own country, it is better to leave political power in the hands of the man who is now exercising it. Interest and understanding are lacking in their attitudes toward works councils and trade unions in their own work experience. A recent survey among Cologne apprentices found that the workers' organizations have to compete strongly for authority with the word of the boss or foreman. [42% of the labor youths polled in Cologne affirmed the necessity of unions; 52% had no opinion on the subject.] This situation is not simply the result of lack of communication between age groups. German youth is growing to maturity at a time when *institutions as well as traditions show an almost total break of continuity.* (Kirchheimer, 1957, p. 185; italics added)

The impact of military devastation and defeat on political behavior may be indicated by the size of the extremist vote following World War II. In nine out of ten European countries holding elections in 1945 or 1946, the Communist party polled the largest share of the total vote in its history. And in these nine countries the Communist vote has not subsequently approached this high-point (the Italian Communist vote was higher in 1953, the only exception).[38]

38. For Austria, Belgium, Denmark, Holland, Norway, Sweden, and Switzerland: statistical yearbooks for each country. For England: McCallum and Readman (1947, pp. 248-52). For France: Finer (1949, p. 336).

The various national Communist parties successfully claimed legitimacy as the most effective source of resistance to the Fascists and their collaborators in those countries where the Fascists had triumphed (Autsria, Belgium, Denmark, France, Holland, Italy, Norway). The Communists were successful in this claim in part because they brought to the resistance (when the needs of Soviet foreign policy required it) "the one experienced clandestine party organization, with its hardened cadres [and] its dedicated energy" (Lorwin, 1954, p. 93). Their success occurred in a context of great social dislocation and confusion, when the symbols of the pre-war social order were blurred or even obliterated. This greatly enhanced the attractiveness of the Communist movement as a vehicle for popular reaction against national humiliation and the failure of the national leadership to defeat the enemy from within as well as without.[39]

In countries experiencing a strong sense of humiliation and defeat the Communist vote shows a sizable increase. France with its Vichyites and Norway with its Quislings are the major cases in point. There also was a very large Communist vote in defeated Italy. And in those countries experiencing a relatively unimpaired sense of national integrity following the war, the Communist vote shows only a small increase (for example, in victorious England and in neutral Switzerland). But the fact that even in these nations the Communist vote reached its height immediately after the war suggests that modern warfare atomizes whole populations and prepares people for mass responses *after* the war as well as during it.

---

39. The successes of the Red Army and of the war-time United Front were additional factors which helped to legitimize the national Communist parties for this role. But these factors do not help to account for differences between nations in this respect.

Summary of Part II

1. There is not a positive relation between the degree of democratization and the extent of mass movements in Western societies (that is, the more democratic countries are not more vulnerable to subversion by mass movements than are the less democratic countries).

a) However, if popular rule is introduced suddenly in a society previously subject to autocratic rule (i.e., without a constitutional heritage), it is likely to engender mass movements which may subvert it.

b) Further, if the growth of independent social groups and classes does not accompany democratization, the lack of multiple centers of power leaves the state unrestrained and unsupported.

2. There probably is not a positive relation between the degree of urbanization and the extent of mass movements in Western societies (for example, the proportion of the population in cities is not positively associated with the proportion of the population engaged in political mass movements).

a) However, if urbanization proceeds at a very rapid rate, especially in its earlier stages it is likely to involve the uprooting of large numbers of people and the failure of new forms of associations to emerge.

b) Further, population movements are more atomizing the greater the social disparity of areas between which the movement takes place. Areas of rapid out-migration as well as those of rapid in-migration may be atomized. Old population elements, as well as new ones, may be atomized. Rapid influx of large numbers of people into organizations makes them more vulnerable to capture by mass-oriented elites.

3. There probably is not a positive relation between the degree of industrialization and extent of mass movements in Western societies (for example, the proportion of the labor force employed in industry is not positively associated with the proportion of the population engaged in political mass movements).

a) However, if industrialization develops at a very rapid rate, especially in its earlier stages it is likely to involve the uprooting of large numbers of people and the failure of new forms of occupational association to emerge.

b) Further, industrialization of the labor force tends to be highly atomizing where industry is confined to large cities and large factories, where workers are recruited directly from the rural population, and where there is little prior development of workingmen's organizations and severe repression of new unions.

4. There appears to be a close relation between the severity of crisis and the extent of mass movements in Western societies.

a) Thus, the more severe the depression in industrial societies, the greater the social atomization, and the more widespread are mass movements (for example, there is a high association between level of unemployment and increase in the extremist electorate).

b) Thus, the stronger a country's sense of national humiliation and defeat in war, the greater the social atomization, and the greater the mass action (for example, there is a close association between military defeat and the rise of strong mass movements).

PART III

SOCIAL COMPOSITION
OF MASS MOVEMENTS

Chapter 9

Social Classes and
Mass Movements

MASS MOVEMENTS depend for their success on the weakness of existing institutions and on the intensive support of large numbers of people. The weakness of organizations in mass society allows them to be penetrated by mass movements. The population then becomes more easily absorbed by means of these captured organizations (as well as by direct mobilization into a movement), including satellite organizations designed to reach unorganized masses. In this section, we shall attempt to account for the kinds of people who flock to mass movements, especially during periods of acute crisis. We seek to show that totalitarian movements in particular mobilize people who are "available" by virtue of being socially alienated.

[A totalitarian movement] depends on two distinct phenomena: on the one hand availability, itself created by a mental break with the milieu, and on the other hand the tendency toward millenarianism or secular religion. These two phenomena do not necessarily go hand in hand: The "available" individuals or groups may be hostile to the Communist message, or on the other hand the appeal of the message may be so great that it creates a break, where none exists. . . . But in general the charm works on men who are already "available" as a result of a break with their milieu. (Aron, 1953, p. 9)

The theory of mass society seeks to account for certain fundamental characteristics of totalitarian movements by contrasting them with established political parties. Thus it views Communist and Fascist movements in terms of their *common* attributes: those which mark them off from genuine parties (including socialist, liberal, and conservative parties). These attributes, as Aron points out in the passage just cited, include a millenarian appeal and the mobilization of available people.

The totalitarian appeal has to be forthcoming, of course, before available people may be mobilized. There is nothing automatic about its presence. It requires the emergence of leaders capable of formulating an ideology and organizing a movement to carry it, as Lenin so well understood in his famous tract, "What Is To Be Done?"[1] In the present study, we restrict ourselves to the task of stating conditions under which people are likely to be responsive to totalitarian leaders. However, even when there are totalitarian leaders capable of exploiting them, these conditions may not be sufficient. People who are responsive to a totalitarian movement at one time may turn to another kind of movement at another time. This proposition is illustrated by the results of a Swedish study which found that similar conditions favored the Communist movement in one area and a religious movement in another area:

Conditions in both of the far-northern counties [of Sweden] were such as to breed radicalism. Both were subject to a rapid rate of colonization and industrial expansion during the past fifty to a hundred years. In both the climate was hard and life was dour. In the one, however, radicalism took a religious form; in the other a political form. (Davison, 1954-55, p. 381)

Furthermore, Swedish public opinion data and census figures show that these two movements recruit similar kinds of people:

---

1. This is a programmatic statement of ideology, agitation, and organization as means for creating and utilizing available masses for the seizure of power.

Both religious radicals and the Communists are far more likely to attract men and young people than are more conservative groups—either religious or political. Here again the Communists and the religious radicals . . . seem to be competing for the allegiance of the same groups. (Davison, 1954-55, p. 382)

The fact that some people turn to religious extremism rather than political extremism is fully compatible with mass theory. But of course the consequences for democracy will be very different depending on which of these alternatives gains a large following.[2] It seems that people are more likely to seize the political alternative during periods of acute crisis. In the following pages, we seek to identify the kinds of people who are especially available for participation in totalitarian movements in such periods.

Up to this point, we have analyzed communism and fascism only insofar as they can be viewed as mass movements. But in order to formulate a fuller explanation of communism and fascism, it is also necessary to treat them as class movements. This means that part of the support for the Communist party is attributable to its being a working-class party, rather than a "mass" movement. Therefore, its social base is in certain respects and under certain conditions similar to that of democratic socialist parties. The analysis of the social base of working-class parties in general, as against those of the middle class, provides understanding that is missed by the analysis of the social base of mass movements in general, as against parties tied to the established order. Mass society theory does not account for the fact that Fascist movements draw their followers disproportionately from the middle classes, and that Communist movements draw their supporters disproportionately from the working classes. It is not contradicted by this class difference between fascism and communism, however, since common mass characteristics may subsist along with differ-

---

2. Political and religious extremism obviously do not exhaust the possibilities of mass deviance. See Merton (1957) for a conceptualization of major modes of deviance.

ent class characteristics. On the contrary, just because fascism and communism are not similar in class composition, we cannot use class theory to account for their similarities, especially their totalitarianism. When organizations have as their central purpose the advancement of class interests, they tend to be restrained and limited by the exigencies of social situations and class traditions. Totalitarian movements, on the other hand, have few stable interests, traditions, or other affiliations of their members to restrain them either in their aims (which tend to be millennial), their methods (which tend to be violent), or control over their members (which tends to be total). Since in this study we are primarily concerned with *similarities* between the political extremes, we are emphasizing mass analysis. But because important *differences* also obtain among these groups, we must utilize class analysis in addition to mass analysis for a fuller description of their social composition.

Mass theory leads to the expectation that the unattached and alienated of all classes are more attracted to extremist symbols and leaders than are their class-rooted counterparts. Since workers tend to be less firmly attached to the social order than are middle-class people, they also tend to be less committed to democratic parties and civil liberties.[3] Thus, in France and Italy, where the working class is poorly related to the social order, Communist movements are large and predominantly proletarian; whereas in Britain and the United States, where the working class is much less isolated from the society, Communist movements are small and ethnic.[4] Middle-class people who lack strong attachments to the community also are more responsive to political extremism than are middle-class people who possess multiple social commitments. Thus, in France and Italy, where cer-

---

3. See Part I, pp. 68-72 above.
4. On the working-class support for the French and Italian Communist parties, see Cantril (1958). On the ethnic composition of the British Communist party, see Pelling (1958, pp. 15-17, 82-3). On the ethnic composition of the American Communist party, see Howe and Coser (1957, pp. 517-8).

tain sections of the middle class are poorly related to the social order, a significant minority of the middle class supports mass movements (e.g., Poujadism in France and neo-Fascism in Italy) ; whereas in Britain and the United States, where the middle class is firmly attached to the social order, middle-class support for mass movements is practically nonexistent (although the Mosley-led Fascists in Britain and the followers of G. L. K. Smith in the U. S., as well as certain sections of McCarthy's followers, constituted such support).

Intellectuals and peasants, small businessmen and industrial workers, when they lack social ties, alike find in the activism and millenarianism of mass movements more promising "solutions" to their plight than they do in the particularistic images of economic interest groups. Thus, mass theory looks to the breakdown of class identities as a critical process whereby people are freed to form new ties based on the commonly shared plight of mass men rather than the mutually exclusive plight of class men. In short, this approach finds in mass men rather than class men the shock troops in large-scale efforts to overturn democratic orders.

Consider the attributes of the early participants in the Nazi movement. They came from every stratum of German society:

Princes without thrones, indebted and subsidized landlords, indebted farmers, virtually bankrupt industrialists, impoverished shopkeepers and artisans, doctors without patients, lawyers without clients, writers without readers, unemployed teachers, and unemployed manual and white-collar workers joined the movement. (Gerth, 1952, p. 105)

Consider the attributes of early participants in the Fascist movement in Italy:

The composition of the Fascist movement also shows its mass-character. The Fascist flag was followed in the beginning by revolutionary syndicalists; by the *Arditi*, who could not forget the war; by discontented demobilized officers, who had no future but to become salesmen; by soldiers; by spirited youths; by loafers and professional criminals; by rich intellectuals who feared the workers, and by desperately poor intellectuals; by a mixture of "patriotic" agrarians, craftsmen and others. . . . *All the various layers of society* were represented, all social groups suspended in this crowd. (Lederer, 1940, pp. 86-7; italics added)

The Communist movement also recruits supporters from the uprooted members of all strata, albeit disproportionately from the working classes.

The following analysis explores the hypothesis that all social classes contribute to the social base of totalitarian movements, and that in particular it is the socially uprooted and unattached members of all classes who support these movements first and in the greatest numbers. This implies that *unattached intellectuals, marginal members of the middle class, isolated industrial and farm workers* have been among the major social types in totalitarian movements.

Chapter 10

Unattached Intellectuals

ANY POLITICAL enterprise that aspires to power will have to command the allegiance of a sizable number of intellectuals and professionals, because their skills are indispensable for its success. Totalitarian movements are no exception in this respect.

A comparison of the backgrounds of Nazi and Soviet leaders suggests the tremendous importance of middle-class intellectuals and professional men in the revolutionary process. . . . Unless a substantial number of them somehow and for some reason become disaffected revolutionaries, there seems to be relatively little danger of revolution. If, on the other hand, their loyalties, beliefs, and interests begin to diverge sharply from established political institutions and values, then the revolutionary dynamism may have been set in motion. (Matthews, 1954, p. 58)

Table 11 shows that (1) in all political elites intellectuals and professionals are over-represented anywhere from four to ten times their proportion of the labor force; (2) they make up a higher proportion of democratic than of totalitarian elites (e.g., the Weimar versus the Nazi cabinet, the French cabinet versus the French Communist party central committee); (3) they make up a higher proportion of the elites than of the rank and file membership of political groups (e.g., 38% of the Fascist cabinet versus 15% of the Fascist party; 34% of CPSU delegates versus 26% of CPSU membership). Hence our problem is to show not that intellectuals *per se* are disposed to support mass movements, but that *certain kinds* of intellectuals under certain conditions are especially susceptible to mass action.

TABLE 11.

Proportion of Political Elites Recruited from the Professions.

POLITICAL GROUP	Professionals (Per Cent)
Democratic groups:	
US Cabinet (1877-1934)	74
US Congress (1949-1951)	69
French Cabinet (1890-1940)	68*
Conservative MPs (1945)	61
House of Commons (1945)	54
Labor MPs (1945)	40
British Cabinet (1916-1935)	44
Weimar Cabinet (1918-1933)	40
Totalitarian groups:	
USSR Central Committee (1922)	40
Fascist Cabinet (1935)	38
CPSU Delegates (1923)	34
SS Elite (about 1940)	32
CP Central Committees (France, Italy, U.S.: 1950)	31‡
Nazi Cabinet (1933-1945)	28
Nazi Elite (1934)	27
CPSU (1923)	26
Nazi Party (1933)	18†
Fascist Party (1921)	15‡

* Per cent of occupations reported.
† Includes merchants and artisans (the proportion of professionals is therefore substantially lower).
‡ Includes students.

SOURCES: U.S.: Matthews (1954, p. 30). England: Matthews (1954, pp. 44, 46). France: Lasswell et al. (1952, p. 30). German cabinets: Knight (1952, p. 30). Nazi elite: Lerner (1951, p. 7). SS elite: Wolfson (n.d., p. 163). Nazi Party: Gerth (1952, p. 106). Fascist cabinet: Lasswell (1947, p. 162). Fascist Party: Finer (1935, p. 143). Communist Party Central Committees: Almond (1954, p. 191). USSR Central Committee and Communist Party: Towster (1948, p. 327).

Intellectuals not only support mass movements; they also originate and promulgate the ideological appeal to fit the mass situation. Those who live for and off symbols—the intellectuals—are least able to suffer a vacuum in the symbolic sphere; at the same time, they are the ones who know how to create the symbols to fill it. *Intellectuals create millennial appeals in response to their own sense of the loss of social*

function and relatedness in the mass society.[5] Their facility
with symbols, plus their commitment to symbolic legitimation for all action, shapes the means they employ. The atomization of masses who possess a sufficient degree of literacy to
receive the intellectuals' messages provides the opportunity
for intellectuals to make common cause with them. These
are the ingredients out of which millenarian mass movements are launched.

Intellectuals do not constitute a politically homogeneous
class in democratic society. Variations in the predisposition
of intellectuals to engage in mass movements appear to be
linked to their level of social integration and responsibility.
*Thus, free-lance intellectuals appear to be more disposed
toward mass movements than intellectuals in corporate
bodies (especially universities).*[6] Among the intellectuals who
gave early support to the American Communist movement,
literary people pre-dominated (Bell, 1952, p. 365). A "second
wave" of intellectuals consisted of slick writers, actors, and
others in entertainment industries who joined during the
Communist Popular Front period. At that time, the strongest
Communist influence and control in organizations of intellectuals and professionals was to be found in Actor's Equity
and the Radio Writer's Guild. After World War II, very
few intellectuals of any kind joined the American Communist party. However, free-lance intellectuals constituted
a larger proportion of the intellectuals in the leadership
group of the major Communist front organization than in
the comparable group of the major anti-communist liberal
organization: 20% of the intellectuals in the Progressive
party's leadership were free-lance, as against only 8% of the

---

5. Of the very large literature dealing with the alienation of intellectuals,
see especially Michels (1949, pp. 316-29); Schumpeter (1947, pp. 145-55);
de Man (1927, pp. 195-237); Hoffer (1951, pp. 129-41); Mills (1951, pp.
142-60); Nomad (1932); Arendt (1951, pp. 318-32); Crossman (1949); Brinton (1952, pp. 42-53); Monnerot (1953, pp. 123-32).

6. This hypothesis is adapted from a lecture given by Professor Edward
Shils at the University of Chicago, 1950.

intellectuals among the leadership of the Americans for Democratic Action.[7] In a recent discussion of "socialism and the intellectuals" in England, Kingsley Amis also suggests that the writer and artist, who are likely to be free-lancers, have manifested a greater affinity for the extreme left, whereas the teacher, for example, has been drawn more to the moderate left:

My own experience at the university in 1941-42 . . . suggests to me that of several possible ways of distinguishing between the Marxist and the non-Marxist, one is especially interesting from our viewpoint. The Marxist wing included a strong faction of the more specifically literary and artistic intellectual which did not appear to the same degree in the democratic-socialist wing: a budding schoolmaster, let us say, was far less likely to be a Marxist than a budding poet was. The same sort of thing held true, I feel, in the world outside the university. (1957, p. 5)

Five reasons may be advanced for the hypothesis that free-lance intellectuals are more receptive to political extremism than are other types of intellectuals. First, the free-lance intellectual, ever since the decline of the patron in the sixteenth and seventeenth centuries, has been dependent on an anonymous and unpredictable market. He has had to start his enterprise anew every generation, and as a result is in an anxiety-arousing position similar to that of the first-generation small businessman. Much more rooted and culturally integrated are those intellectuals who enter into old and stable organizations, such as the university. Second, free-lance intellectuals tend to have fewer institutional responsibilities than intellectuals in professional organizations, and therefore are less likely to be committed to central institutions. Third, rewards are much less certain to be forthcoming for the free-lance intellectual, the form of the reward less predictable, and the permanence of the recognition more tenuous. In particular, the degree of correspondence between expecta-

7. These data were compiled by the author from appropriate volumes of *Who's Who in America.*

tions and realizations, the extent to which expectations are stable and conventional, and rewards predictable, is greater for the academic man. Fourth, free-lance intellectuals (e.g., writers and journalists) tend to be more dependent on their audience, over which they have relatively little control, and to feel greater social distance from it, in contrast to, for example, the professor in relation to his students. Fifth, free-lance intellectuals suffer more when there is an over-supply of intellectuals. Many go into free-lancing when the professions are overcrowded.[8] In general, a condition of chronic overcrowding of the professions engenders large numbers of discontented and alienated intellectuals of all kinds. This was the situation in Germany following World War I.

The abnormal increase in attendance at German universities and professional colleges began even before the depression, as a result of the denial to tens of thousands of access to commercial occupations. The university became a haven of refuge for individuals who otherwise would sink to the ranks of the unemployed. After 1926, perhaps 30% of

---

8. In this connection Geiger (1949, pp. 118-9) has argued that "those less qualified aspirants for practical-academic positions, especially those who have not even succeeded in passing their exams, will attempt to make their way as 'free intelligentsia.' Journalism was (and in part still is) a preferred refuge for such types. . . . To fill the demands of a practical-academic profession, a specified and measurable amount of knowledge is required. The entrance into the free intelligentsia is not subject to such a control. There are no exams nor minimum qualifications. The beginning is made at one's own risk, and the future career depends on success only. Only after some time can it be said that the aspirant has succeeded or been a failure. The ultimate proof of incapacity lies in the far future, to which one can close one's eyes. And besides even in the case of ultimate and unequivocal failure, one always has the excuse that the market and the public are incapable to judge. One is a misunderstood genius. A pseudo-intelligentsia of this type tends to appear in greater numbers in a depression, where the number in academic study is unhealthily large. The flight from the limited opportunities in the economy not only increases the number of young academics beyond the demand for them, but is constituted mainly by weak vocations and people of little energy. They are the first who are discouraged by increased competition." (Quotation supplied by Juan Linz.) Geiger's remarks suggest the importance of a sixth reason why academicians are less susceptible to the appeals of mass movements, namely, the greater rigor of their intellectual training and their critical habits of thought.

the German students entered the university for this reason. The expected number of unemployed university graduates for 1934 was estimated at 90,000 (Doerne, 1932, pp. 66-8). The resulting difficulties in rationally planning a life-career increased irrational responses, including susceptibility of students and intellectuals to a belief in cure-alls.[9] "It was students and unemployed graduates who furnished numbers, leaders, enthusiasm and fanaticism to the National Socialist fighting organizations" (Hoover, 1933, p. 26).[10]

The susceptibility of university-trained people in Germany to totalitarian appeals is shown by the fact that *one-fourth* of the SS elite had previously received the doctorate. Elections to the student councils in German universities from 1929 to 1931 also bear out this point (Bracker, 1955, pp. 146-9). They show that the Nazis were much stronger among the students than in the middle-class population as a whole. In the student council elections in the academic year 1930-31, the Nazis secured half or more of the vote in nine of the eighteen universities for which data exist, and 40% or more in fourteen of these universities. Nazi penetration was facilitated by the general political apathy prevailing in the student organizations. Primary resistance to the Nazis came from dominantly Catholic universities, since here was a strong value-system and social organization to counter the Nazi appeal.

Not only students, but the younger generation as a whole was much more highly represented in the Nazi party than in the Social Democratic party or in the population at large (see Table 12). "The Nazi party could truthfully boast of being a 'young party' " (Gerth, 1952, p. 107).[11]

The way in which the threat—or the actuality—of being

9. See Mannheim (1940, p. 104).
10. Cf. Kotschnig (1937, pp. 117-9, 175); Heiden (1944, pp. 28-9); Lerner (1952, pp. 32-3).
11. Cf. Heiden (1944, p. 351): "With these young people came a new human type: the man who could not and did not want to be counted among any definite social class ... it had never had a class." See also Anderson (1945, p. 147); Bendix (1952, p. 369); S. Neumann (1942, p. 30).

TABLE 12.

Age-Composition of the Nazi and Socialist Parties, Germany, 1931.

AGE	Nazis	SPD	Germany (1933)
18-30	38%	19%	31%
31-40	28	27	22
41-50	20	27	17
50+	15	27	30
Total	101%	100%	100%

SOURCE: Gerth (1952, p. 108).

declassed favors the development of totalitarian attitudes is illustrated by the response of German engineers to nazism. Speier has observed that the superordinate position of the university-trained engineer vis-à-vis the graduate of a technical trade school was shaken considerably by the depression, since it led to the downgrading (some even took jobs as manual workers) or unemployment of academic engineering graduates. "We therefore find the interesting picture of the *Butib,* as the most prominent organization of the technical employees, with the majority of its members among trade school graduates, pursuing a very vigorous trade union policy with a socialist trend, while *the younger generation of graduate engineers, fresh from the technical colleges, more readily becomes National Socialist than other university men"* (1939, pp. 44-5, italics added). This tendency toward mass action on the part of the university engineers during the depression was facilitated by their normal lack of organization, and by their normal lack of interest in and knowledge about politics, so that the loss of function resulting from unemployment sharply increased their susceptibility to Nazi appeals.

Another example is provided by the demobilized German army officer turned Nazi. Many of the lower officers were "intellectuals in uniform," having been recruited from among the ranks of university students of upper-middle-class background. Following the First World War, "they found no career and no bread in the breakdown after the peace, their officer days remained for many the high point in their existence; the hope for a return of the golden days remained their secret consolation" (Heiden, 1944, p. 29). Remaining officers at heart, they identified their personal sense of superfluousness with the humiliation of national defeat, and blamed both on the new democratic republic (Bullock, 1952, p. 53). It was but a short step from demobilization to remobilization in the para-military bands which sprung up in the 1920's and provided the cadres of the National Socialist movement. The advent of the depression swelled the ranks of declassed intellectuals with unemployed university graduates, who made common cause with the lower officers turned Nazi: "the 40,000 or 50,000 workless university graduates in 1931-33 became, together with unemployed subalterns of the old imperial army, the spearhead of the National Socialist movement" (Kotschnig, 1937, p. 175). Heiden emphasized the role of the declassed intellectual in the rise of Nazism in his phrase "the armed bohemians": "From the wreckage of dead classes arises the new class of intellectuals, and at the head march the most ruthless, those with the least to lose, hence the strongest: the armed bohemians, to whom war is home and civil war fatherland" (1944, p. 100).

It may be noted in passing that certain kinds of intellectuals tend to be hypersensitive to their nation's power, and to express that feeling through affiliation with "tough" movements. This tendency has a long history in both Germany and Russia. There was a conflict between Western-oriented and Germanic intellectuals during the nineteenth and early twentieth century, the former following France as a model and supporting democratic and socialist tendencies (many were Jews), the latter having a militaristic and nationalistic Germany as a model and supporting anti-Western (especially anti-French) and anti-Semitic values (Mann, 1955, p. 48). A similar conflict between the Westernizers and xenophobes characterized Russian intellectuals during the same period and with parallel alignments (e.g., Westernizers looked to France as a model, included many Jews; Slavophiles eschewed France in favor of a glorified Russia, were anti-Semitic). There is one very significant difference, however. Whereas the Germanic intellectuals gravitated toward "tough" movements on the right, especially Nazism, Slavophiles gravitated toward the extreme left, especially Bolshevism — while in both cases the so-called Westernizers tended toward a more moderate position, particularly democratic socialism (Wolfe, 1948, p. 23).

Russian conditions were even more favorable than the German situation for the development of an intellectual vanguard of a mass movement, because the Russian intelligentsia did not, like its German counterpart, possess social roots in the commercial bourgeoisie and therefore was even more susceptible to the lure of messianic symbols. Thus, the Bolshevik movement initially was constituted by intellectuals to a much greater extent than was the early Nazi movement. Prior to the Provisional Government which had opened the way for participation by intellectuals in government, the Tsarist regime had rejected them totally, depriving them of their chance to share in power and making of them "superfluous men" aware that their aspirations, talents, and knowledge were of no avail in the nation's life (Fainsod, 1953, p. 6). Furthermore, Russian universities created a swollen intelligentsia whom the Tsarist government was unwilling to integrate into a society urgently in need of their services. From these intellectuals came the "professional revolutionaries" of the Bolshevik movement. "Lenin's revolution is essentially not a proletarian revolution, it is 'the revolution' of the intelligentsia" (Borkenau, 1938, p. 44).

The German and Russian experiences suggest the general proposition that *the more isolated the intellectuals from their society, the more revolutionary and messianic their outlook.* Social isolation of intellectuals not only breeds resentment against the whole structure of society; it also leads to their *remoteness* from the day-to-day interests of people (especially workers) whom intellectuals seek to mobilize against the existing order—a remoteness which removes any checks on the intellectuals that might arise from among their followers. Thus it is that intellectuals are especially attracted to movements which themselves are isolated and remote from society, for this kind of movement allows free rein to the messianic tendencies of alienated intellectuals, and provides the opportunity to indulge in abstract problems of doctrine rather than practical considerations of politics. The converse also appears to be true; intellectuals tend to push movements toward abstract and remote concerns.

A study of American intellectuals who were active Communists found a marked contrast between them and American trade union officials who also participated in the Communist party: "In comparison with trade unionists, the intellectuals were more concerned with defiance of authority, excitement, and feelings of belonging to an elite group." The pronounced social isolation of intellectuals as compared to trade unionists is evidenced by the fact that none of the former had belonged to any organizations prior to joining the party. It would appear from this study that the labor leaders, in their desire to advance concrete trade union interests, found the party's isolation oppressive; whereas the intellectuals were attracted to the party in part *because* it was so far outside the established order (Krugman, 1952).

The mass movement in its early phase of development must rely primarily on the agitational and propaganda skills of its leaders to build up a following and a set of ideal values to sustain that following, whereas a mature mass movement is more likely to have become rationalized into an administrative organization emphasizing operational effectiveness rather than symbolic attractiveness. Hence, the younger movement appeals more to the intellectuals, as it gives them a more useful and prestigeful role to perform. The Bolshevik movement illustrates this:

The revolution of 1917 [in Russia] was led and organized by brilliant, young intellectuals from a middle-class background. In the course of the establishment of the Soviet State, the need for such people diminished, and they were gradually replaced by less colorful but efficient administrators and organizers. This shift is illustrated, at the top, by the change in leadership from Lenin to Stalin. (Schueller, 1951, p. 42)

The Nazi movement is another case in point. As compared with later Nazi leaders, the earlier ones were more likely to be intellectuals. The SS elite, which increased its power after 1934, included proportionately fewer specialists in symbols (writers, journalists, professors, etc.) than did the earlier Nazi elite (Wolfson, n. d., p. 164).

In summary, intellectuals are more likely to join and lead mass movements seeking to supplant a democratic order when they are socially isolated. Free-lance intellectuals, as compared with those who are attached to institutions, have fewer relations to the social order, and their lack of corporate relations leaves them less restrained by that order. Therefore, they are more inclined toward mass movements. Intellectuals are more easily mobilized into isolated mass movements (e.g., movements in their early period of formation), since such movements are more likely to give them status and scope for the expression of their alienation. They are more likely to enter mass movements during periods of severe overcrowding of the professions, since the resulting underemployment or unemployment snaps their already precarious ties to society and transforms latent disaffection into total rejection.

Chapter 11

Marginal Middle Classes

ANY POLITICAL enterprise which aspires to power on the basis of popular support will have to command the allegiance of sizable numbers of people from both the middle and working classes, because the size of these classes makes it a necessity. This is true even when a political group depends for primary support upon only one class.

As Table 13 shows, the Republican party receives disproportionate support from the middle class; but at the same time, a large minority of its votes is cast by workers (note the large increase in the proportion of the Republican vote coming from workers in that party's victory in 1952). By the same token, the Democratic party requires large numbers of middle-class votes to turn its working-class majority into a national majority. In England, too, the Conservative party depends on workers for a large share of its votes. The Labor party commands proportionately many fewer middle-class votes, but that is one of its major electoral problems.

Political mass movements are no exceptions to this rule. The French Communists receive thirty per cent of their electoral support from middle-class voters, according to a survey taken in 1952. The Italian Communist-Nenni Socialist coalition also depends on middle-class voters for about one-third of its electoral base. Although no figures are available on the composition of the Communist voters in the United States, one study (Almond, 1954, p. 189) reports that the party's membership is over one-half middle-class (including students; if students are excluded, the proportion is a bit under one-half). McCarthy had no political organization, but his following constituted an incipient mass movement which had considerable working-class support. A Gallup poll taken in March, 1954, found 45% of manual workers expressing a favorable opinion of McCarthy. The neo-Fascists in Italy obtain about one-third of their support from the working class (urban and rural). It is more difficult to estimate the proportion of Nazi votes which are attributable to workers in Hitler's successful bid for power, but the composition of the party in 1933 was well over one-third urban and rural workers (Gerth, 1952, p. 106). The same is true for the Italian Fascist party in 1921 (Finer, 1935, p. 143).

TABLE 13.

Class Composition of Electorate of Parties in Several Countries.

PARTY	Per Cent of Party Electorate Who Are	
	Middle Class	Working Class
United States (1952)		
Republican	63	37
Democratic	41	59
United States (1948)		
Republican	76	24
Democratic	40	60
Great Britain (1951)		
Conservative	51	49
Labor	14	86
Germany (1955)		
Christian Democratic	60	40
Social Democratic	28	72
France (1952)		
Gaullist	68	32
MRP (Catholic)	74	26
Socialist	52	48
Communist	30	70
Italy (1953)		
Fascist	66	34
Christian Democratic	70	30
Social Democratic	69	31
Communist, Left Socialist	37	63

SOURCES: Data recomputed from University of Michigan Survey Research Center surveys of 1948 and 1952 (U.S.); Bonham (1954, p. 168); Janowitz (1958, p. 22); Williams (1954, p. 446); and "Italian Political Party Preferences" (1953). The distinction between working class and middle class in this table is essentially one between manual and non-manual occupations.

Fascist movements, then, are not adequately conceived as middle-class phenomena, nor are Communist movements to be understood merely as working-class phenomena. In the latter case, in addition to the figures just given, we may recall that middle-class intellectuals have played a decisive role in Communist movements, everywhere providing leadership for nascent Communist parties. In the former case not only do Fascist movements rely on working-class support for a significant portion of their following; but in at least one instance (the Peronista), a Fascist-like movement had a predominantly working-class base; and in another instance (Italian fascism) the original cadres (led by Mussolini) came out of the socialist movement.

These observations suggest that what from the standpoint of class analysis is the "deviant" portion of a totalitarian party's social base (e.g., the working class vote for a Fascist party) is from the standpoint of mass analysis an expression of its basic character. The fact remains, however, that even though there is a "totalitarian appeal" common to both movements, fascism has a greater affinity for the middle classes and communism for the working classes. We shall not attempt to analyze this class differential here (it has been described in numerous studies), nor more broadly how dispositions to engage in mass movements get channelized along the lines of one extreme or the other. What we are after is the identification of kinds of people who support mass movements of whatever kind. Therefore, in this section on the middle classes, support for Fascist and proto-Fascist movements will be used as the main indicator of mass susceptibility; and in the following section on the working classes, support for Communist movements will be used in a similar fashion.

We wish to show that there are marked similarities between the condition of middle-class people who support mass (especially Fascist) movements and the condition of working-class people who support mass (especially Communist) movements. The similarity of condition is one of mass availability resulting from lack of social integration. Thus, it is the more marginal sections of the middle classes which manifest the greater susceptibility to mass movements; specifically, poorly-established business rather than well-established business, and small business rather than big business.

Marginal Big Business

Since big business in highly developed capitalist systems tends to possess a network of organizations for the defense of its interests, as well as a high involvement in voluntary associations of all kinds, its willingness to risk the destruction of an existing democratic order should, in the ordinary course of events, be relatively low. For its multiple stakes in that order require, among other things, that big business protect its position by maintaining continuous access to policy-making institutions, and this access would be jeopardized by support of extremist movements unless they gave strong promise of success.

The attitudes of capitalist groups toward the policy of their nations are predominantly adaptive rather than causative, today more than ever. Also, they hinge to an astonishing degree on short-run considerations equally remote from any deeply laid plans and from any definite "objective" class interests. (Schumpeter, 1947, p. 55) [12]

This argument, of course, is diametrically opposed to the Marxist theory of fascism, which claims to find in the most highly organized business groups the main impetus and base for fascism. The fact that the most highly developed capitalist societies have experienced the smallest Fascist movements and the strongest commitments to democratic values on the

---

12. Schumpeter adds that "at this point Marxism degenerates into the formulation of popular superstitions."

part of the business community, and that it has been in the less industrial countries (e.g., Italy) and in countries in which the state assumed a major responsibility for industrial development (e.g., Germany) that Fascist movements have been strong and have commanded at least some important business support, sharply contradicts the Marxist theory. Furthermore, within countries that went Fascist, it was the less established business groups that backed Fascist movements earlier and with greater vigor.

National Socialism received little big business support in its initial period, but picked up considerable aid from this source during its rapid growth following the depression. Prior to the depression, when the movement was small and weak, what little support was forthcoming from big business centered in the local South German producers. Nationwide industrial leaders were not much interested in sponsoring the Nazis until after 1928 (Hallgarten, 1952, p. 225). "The German economy did not raise up Hitler. . . . To be sure, he did approach big capital—though as a blackmailer, not as a lackey. But in that springtime of self-confidence [prior to the depression], there was nothing to be had from capital by blackmail" (Heiden, 1944, p. 264). This matter of the timing of big business support for the Nazis is an important one, for it is one thing to latch on to an already successful totalitarian party for opportunistic reasons, and quite another ardently to cast one's lot with a young and struggling movement of highly uncertain outcome. If nazism were indeed to be understood as the "last stand of capitalism," big business would not have withheld its support until the Nazis achieved more power than the conservatives. In Germany, and elsewhere when Fascist parties have triumphed, big business does not so much *create* these totalitarian movements as it attempts to use them once they are ascendant. In general, "the evidence . . . will not support those who attribute to German industrialists (. . . with noteworthy exceptions) a dynamic role in the advent of National Socialism" (Almond, 1957, p. 198).

If big business for the most part did not rally early to Hitler, neither did it support the Republic (Bullock, 1952, p. 57). By 1930, however, faced with great pressures on their economic position and confronted with a powerful Nazi movement, portions of big business did give considerable financial backing to Hitler. What is of specific note for the present analysis is the apparent fact that this support did not emanate from big business as a whole, but from its newer sections. "It would appear that the old industrial families of the Ruhr feared Hitler's budding totalitarianism much more strongly than did the directors of the anonymous companies who live on big salaries, instead of on individual profits" (Hallgarten, 1952, p. 243).

Thus, although before 1930 apparently no central organ of industry made financial contributions to the Nazis,[13] and at no time *before* the Nazi victory does it seem that German industry as a whole or as an organized group supported nazism, those large contributions which were forthcoming by 1930, and which played a crucial role in the following years, came particularly from leaders of heavy industry, especially steel.[14] This was the sector of German business which developed late and failed to achieve an autonomous position in the economic order. Heavy industry was more strongly affected by the authoritarianism of the Prussian monarchy than the rest of the middle classes, "because its period of rapid expansion coincided with the consolidation of the Bismarck Reich and was made possible in considerable part by the protectionist and armament policies of that regime. . . . On the condition that it accept a subordinate role in this authoritarian bureaucratic regime, heavy industry was given the advantages of a large, protected internal market, the prospect of social acceptance by the aristocracy and court, and gratification of national pride through the rapid rise to power of the second Reich" (Almond, 1957, pp. 195-6).

---

13. See Peterson (1954, pp. 112-17).
14. See Thyssen (1941, p. 102). Thyssen (in 1932) made the largest financial contribution to the Nazis.

This orientation encouraged militant resistance to union-ization and active support of extreme national groups such as the Pan-German League prior to the war, and opposition to the Weimar Republic after the war. When the depression hit, several of the big industrial concerns that faced the greatest economic difficulties began to pour large sums of money into the Nazi organization (Hallgarten, 1952, p. 245). While some were looking for a "savior," most were more calculating in their support of nazism. The latter, according to a leading conservative who himself at first cooperated with Hitler, believed that nazism was a patron of order and security that would help restore profits.

The restoration of "order," the disciplining of the workers, the ending of politically fixed wages and profit-destroying social services, the abolition of the workers' freedom of association, and the replacing of the continual alteration of short-lived parlia-mentary governments by a stable political system that permits long-range calculation—all these things tempt leaders of indus-try and finance and of society to shut their eyes to the funda-mental difference between the true motives with which the dy-namic dictatorships are set up and the motives which lead the conservative elements to support them. (Rauschning, 1939, pp. 105-6)

Even among those large industrialists who supported the Nazis, there were many who did not fully close their eyes, and who were fearful lest they be totally absorbed by the Nazi movement. In consequence, part of their objective in supporting Hitler was to restrain him, particularly on eco-nomic matters (Lochner, 1954, p. 20). The better part of the big industrial concerns, "while welcoming Hitler as an ally against labor, would have preferred him being used as a mere tool in the hands of a cabinet controlled by industry and the Junkers" (Hallgarten, 1952, p. 245). Some cautious industrialists, to be on the safe side, continued their mem-bership in other political parties while quietly acquiring membership in the Nazi party (Lochner, 1954, pp. 22-3) .[15] In general, it would appear that big businessmen were more opportunistic toward nazism than the other classes were, since they had the greater stake in preserving the existing economic order; at the same time, newer sections of big business, having less at stake than the old industrial families, rallied to Hitler's side once his ascendancy became apparent.

An old and rooted upper class, with established traditions, tends to strike an attitude of *noblesse oblige* toward the disinherited, and to seek accommodation via amalgamation rather than subversion of the system. The new rich, on the other hand, when faced with great pressures on their position in the existing order, more often will support extremist movements. In the United States, the little support which Huey Long received from the wealthy came from "mavericks of one sort or another who 'did not belong' because of their ancestry, the sources of their money, or their accent" (Key, 1949, p. 163). McCarthy also was supported by newly wealthy individuals (e.g., Texas oil millionaires) during a period of prolonged prosperity. At such times, all social barriers to the power and prestige of new fortunes are felt to be great shackles imposed by the old upper class. In general, new wealth is more liable to make common cause with the disaffected of all classes, since it is rootless (Lipset, 1955, p. 195).

Marginal Small Business

Big business as a whole occupies a central position in industrial democracies, and therefore except for its more

---

15. Among the Reichstag members in 1928 connected with I. G. Farben, one sat with the DNVP, one with the DDP, and one with the Center party. I. G. Farben contributed to all these parties, and later to the Nazis (Lewinson, 1930, pp. 84-5) .

marginal elements has not been especially attracted to mass movements. Small business, on the other hand, increasingly is marginal in modern society and as a result has been more susceptible to mass movements. Small business is less and less assimilated into a world of rationalized enterprise, but it also cannot find security in a declining world of individual enterprise. Squeezed between the pressures of big business and big labor, the class interests of small business are inherently ambiguous, finding allies neither in the classes above nor in the classes below. The central difficulty facing small business is the relative absence of realistic possibilities for improving its long-run economic position in a world increasingly dominated by large-scale organization. Big business finds bureaucratic organization congruent with its interests; and industrial workers have ready recourse to trade-union organization as a counter to big business organization. Even white-collar employees increasingly have the possibility of using collective means to protect their interests, as their conditions of work become rationalized (for example, as office workers are massed together in large numbers, and as their work is standardized, more of them join unions). But the small businessman faces much greater difficulty in rationalizing his enterprise or his relations with other small businessmen. He is truly the marginal man in the industrialized society, and therefore he is readily available for nihilistic mass movements.

There is widespread agreement among students of anti-democratic movements that small businessmen contributed substantial support to the Fascists in Italy, the Nazis in Germany, the Poujadists in France, and the McCarthyists in America. Considering first the Italian Fascists, it has been established that three-fourths of the provincial party secretaries came from the lesser bourgeoisie (Lasswell, 1947, p. 161). But the lower-middle class did not respond uniformly to the appeals of fascism. The *urban* sections figured more prominently in the leadership and active cadres of the

Fascist movement. Furthermore, it was the more marginal and unintegrated members of the urban lower-middle class who provided the bulk of active members. These were people who remained outside of the established middle-class organizations, and therefore were "ready to rush in any direction" (Rossi, 1938, pp. 340-2).

In post-war Italy, artisans in business for themselves have given less support to the democratic parties than have other middle-class groups (see Table 14).

TABLE 14.—Preference for Anti-Democratic Parties by Type of Middle-Class Occupation, Italy, 1953.

	AMONG THOSE WHO ARE			
PER CENT WHO PREFER	Free Artisans	White Collar	Employers	Professionals or Executives
Anti-democratic parties	52	36	24	16
Fascists	14	11	11	—
Monarchists	14	18	7	8
Nenni Socialists	15	2	6	8
Communists	9	5	—	—
Democratic parties	48	64	76	84
Total	100%	100%	100%	100%

SOURCE: Data recomputed from "Italian Political Party Preferences" (1953, p. 12).

Small businessmen also contributed much more than their share to Hitler's mass base. These self-employed members of the lower-middle class felt themselves squeezed between the industrial workers and industrialists, "whose unions, cartels, and parties took the center of the stage" (Lasswell, 1933, p. 374). The Nazis responded directly to the small businessman's resentments by attacking those features of industrialism that were most threatening to small business. Following their accession to power, however, the Nazis terminated their support of small business, since they had no interest in deliberately limiting the opportunities for industrial growth and large-scale distribution (Schweitzer, 1955, pp. 580-82).

Another section of the middle class that disproportionately supported the Nazis consisted of the lower white-collar employees. This is evidenced by the growth of anti-democratic and pro-Nazi organizations of white-collar people, and the concomitant decline in white-collar organizations that favored democracy (Gay, 1952, pp. 209-11).[16] White-collar support for Hitler cannot be accounted for in the same terms as small business support, since white-collar employees are not marginal to large-scale enterprise. Rather, it would appear to be based on resentment against a system which failed to fulfill its promises of status and security within rationalized organization. In other words, white-collar people appear to have reacted more to the *crisis* of industrial capitalism than to the *order* of industrial capitalism, whereas small businessmen reacted against the order itself (Trow, 1958, pp. 278-9). Thus, white-collar people have not generally responded to mass appeals except during the depression (and then in only a few countries), whereas small businessmen have on certain occasions responded to mass appeals even during periods of relative prosperity. Poujadism and McCarthyism are two recent examples of this.

Poujade fashioned a large if amorphous movement out of the resentment of small businessmen against the representatives of modernization, especially big business, big labor, and big government. Yet salaried employees not only rejected the movement; they have constituted a favorite target for Poujade, who complained bitterly against their social security, family allocations, and other economic gains (Hoffmann, 1956, p. 28). Poujadism in its initial and primary face is the revolt of merchants and artisans residing in small towns and rural areas, lacking organizations of their own to protect their interests, and taking a dim view of all political parties. The first adherents and local directors by and large were small merchants or artisans, who, in the words of one of the earliest militants of the movement, "were tired, dis-

---

16. Cf. F. Neumann (1936, p. 20).

couraged, without hope, without anything . . . who worked harder and longer than before the war and than their parents did but who lost ground rather than advanced."[17] Thus, out of the 52 Poujadists elected in 1956, 26 are merchants and the other 26 are either artisans or heads of small or medium enterprises, plus a school director and two students (Hoffmann, 1956, p. 190).

The Poujadists have been strongest in those areas which have benefited least by the modernization of French economic life. Poujadists gained their major electoral success in the economically stagnant south and west of France, and have had very little appeal in those regions where industrialization has developed furthest. Within departments, Poujadists generally have succeeded better in the rural cantons than in the urban and industrial ones. Poujadism is rooted in marginal areas and supported by marginal members of the middle classes; for it has flourished in those areas by-passed in the rationalization of French society and among those people who have been most frustrated by this process. Poujade succeeded above all in mobilizing unorganized sections of the rural middle classes in the backward Center and Midi.[18] The marginality characteristic of Poujade's adherents is linked to the mass behavior of the movement: its reliance on direct action (exemplified in the physical resistance to tax collections), anti-parliamentarism, and early collaboration with the Communists (a collaboration apparently so thorough that when Poujade broke with the Communists he complained "they went so far as to tell me what I must say") ; in some areas the Communists supplied the leadership of the Poujadist movement, and even many of the voters (Hoffmann, 1956, pp. 38-40).

In prosperous post-war America, there is some evidence to indicate that it also has been the small businessman rather than the white-collar employee who voices support for Mc-

---

17. Quoted by Hoffmann (1956, p. 36).
18. See pp. 148-49 above.

Carthyism, another mass movement with certain anti-demo-cratic overtones. A study of the social base of McCarthy in Bennington, Vermont, in 1954 (the height of McCarthy's popularity) reports that less than 30% of salaried employees approved of McCarthy, as compared with over 50% of the small businessmen (Trow, 1958, p. 278). What is of special note is the finding that the small businessmen were much more favorable to McCarthy than white-collar people of *similar education*. This is to say that the difference is truly one of occupation and not merely an artifact of the lower educational level of small businessmen.

TABLE 15.—Support for McCarthy by Occupation and Education.

LESS THAN HIGH SCHOOL GRADUATES		HIGH SCHOOL GRADUATES		SOME COLLEGE OR MORE	
Small Business	White Collar	Small Business	White Collar	Small Business	White Collar
65%	38%	58%	36%	32%	22%
N (52)	(53)	(38)	(78)	(44)	(124)

SOURCE: Trow (1958, p. 274).

Table 15 shows that education does make an important difference in level of support for McCarthy, especially as between those who have been to college and those who have not. Among both small businessmen and white-collar employees, support for McCarthy decreases as education increases. But the differences between these two occupational groups remain, even on the college level. A clue to the source of these differences between small businessmen and salaried workers of similar education is provided by an analysis of their attitudes toward the growth of large-scale organization. The Bennington study shows that small businessmen are more likely than are people in other occupations to believe that *both* big companies and labor unions have too much power. Among those with less than four years of high school, 41% of the small businessmen but only 25% of the salaried employees and 29% of the manual workers believe that both big business and labor have too much power. It is among the small businessmen who hold such beliefs that McCarthy receives overwhelming approval: almost 3 out of 4 in this subgroup were McCarthy supporters. "Here is evidence that a generalized fear of the dominant currents and institutions of modern society was an important source of McCarthy's mass appeal, not *only* among small businessmen, but perhaps especially among a group like small businessmen whose economic and status security is continually threatened by those currents and institutions" (Trow, 1958, p. 277).

In sum, small businessmen have provided strong support for fascism, nazism, Poujadism, and McCarthyism. However, it does not follow that these movements themselves may be understood simply as expressions of small business. Mass movements, especially Fascist movements, acquire much wider support than that supplied by one occupational grouping alone. This may be shown by a consideration of the role of the farmer in the rise of mass movements.

Marginal Farmers

Differences between large farmers and small farmers parallel in part those which have been observed to obtain between big businessmen and small businessmen. Small farmers tend to back both communism and fascism to a greater extent than do large farmers. In both France and Italy, the poorer the farmer the higher the support for the Communist party; and small farmers in Italy support the neo-Fascists twice as frequently as do the large farmers (Stoetzel, 1955, p. 118; *Italian Political Party Preferences*, 1953, p. 12). In Germany, a major source of support for National Socialism was the small, independent family farmer rather than the large landowner. An ecological study of voting in Schleswig-Holstein, the only election district in which the Nazis obtained a majority of the valid votes cast in the July, 1932, election, found a positive correlation between the proportion of people employed on small farms and the percentage of votes received by the Nazis in 1932. At the same time, large landowners were found to be less inclined to vote Nazi and more to vote Conservative (Heberle, 1951, pp. 228-30). Studies of other regions in Germany reveal similar patterns of Nazi strength among small rather than large farmers.[19]

It is not only the worse economic position of small farmers, compared with large farmers, which creates their greater affinity for mass movements. It is also their *group isolation* and the *alienation* from society which this isolation breeds. Where farmers lose their ties to the larger social order, they are more available for extremist movements. Thus, a factor which favored the success of Hitler among the small farmers was the relative paucity of social relations between people living on small farms *and* the larger society (farmers were likely to have multiple ties *within* a farming area). Where intermediate relations existed, nazism was less successful. In Bavaria, for example, farmers organized by the Catholics (as well as workers organized by the Socialists) were relatively immune to the appeals of nazism (Loomis and Beagle, 1946).

In critical situations, smaller and poorer farmers often back the political extremes rather than the democratic parties, in part because they lack established organizations and leaders to summon their loyalties. Table 16 shows that while one-half of the wealthy farmers in the United States belong to one or more agricultural organizations, only about one-eighth of the poor farmers have any such affiliation. Even the populist Farmer's Union has, if anything, a higher proportion of wealthy members than do the more conservative Bureau and Grange. In farmer-run organizations in other countries, the wealthier producers also are more active

19. See Loomis and Beagle (1946).

TABLE 16.—Membership in Farm Organizations by Economic Level of Farmers, United States, 1943.

ECONOMIC LEVEL	PER CENT BELONGING TO				
	Farm Bureau	Grange	Farmers Union	Other	None
High	30	5	6	16	50
Medium	18	4	1	8	71
Low	6	2	1	4	87
Total	18	3	2	9	71

SOURCE: Cantril (1951, p. 5).

than the poorer farmers. In France, for example, the confederation of farmers has been faced with loss of membership among small holders and tenants (Wright, 1953). Peasants who have turned to the Communists in France lack their own leaders, since leadership in agricultural organizations has fallen to the more prosperous farmers (Ehrmann, 1952, p. 41). In the villages of Russia in 1917, an inferior political consciousness born of non-participation in the larger society permitted the peasants to be swayed one way and the other, depending on the intensity and persistence of pressure applied by the various competing movements. "Apparently often there was a herd and it did stampede" (Radkey, 1950, pp. 70-1).

Extremism among farmers is associated with their isolation ". . . from the larger body politic. . . . They do not command the established means of communications" (S. Neumann, 1942, pp. 98-100). The loss of contact with centers of power and communication accompanying the rise of the city has bred agrarian antagonism to symbols of urban preeminence and it has encouraged glorification of the rural past. The first readily has been transformed into anti-Semitism; and the latter easily is perverted into ethnocentric, extremist politics (much as religious revivalism first began in rural areas in part as a reaction against urbane religion). Thus the Nazi glorification of rural living and the *volk*, as well as Nazi hostility toward the Jews and finance capitalism, was highly congenial to German peasants. Furthermore, "the rural population constitutes the compact mass which stands behind the uncompromising emotional nationalism. That is perhaps the most important reason why movements like National Socialism and fascism are first of all supported by the peasants" (Friedrich, 1937, pp. 60-1). Anti-Semitism and anti-urbanism were also manifested by rural movements in North America, including the Populist party and the Social Credit party.

Poorer farmers have been especially receptive to xenophobic appeals because they have not been very successful in forging new ties to replace those relations which were eroded by urbanization. Wealthier farmers, on the other hand, have been more fully integrated into urban society. Comparison of twentieth century with nineteenth century America reveals this change. In the nineteenth century nearly all farmers were inevitably isolated; but with the widespread diffusion in the last fifty years of the automobile, radio, telephone, mail order purchasing, and the like, the well-to-do farmers have become able to participate in the same cultural milieu as their urban counterparts. But if the rapid development of communication and transportation has pulled the wealthier farmer into the mainstream of society, it has left much less of a mark on the poorer farmer. "With these changes there has developed in the American countryside a disparity in living standards and outlook between the most affluent and the least privileged that almost matches anything the city has to show" (Hofstadter, 1955, p. 128). Therefore, the poorer and more isolated farmers, like their counterparts in business, are especially vulnerable to the appeal of the demagogue. Huey Long, Talmadge, and Bilbo, for example, gained their main following from among small farmers rather than large farmers in the South.[20]

In conclusion, the middle classes are not uniformly vulnerable to the appeal of mass movements. The *old* middle

20. See Heberle and Bertrand (1949) and Key (1949).

classes, both urban and rural, are more vulnerable than the *new* middle classes; and the *lower* middle classes are more vulnerable than the *upper* middle classes. Mass theory helps to account for these differences by adding to the economic factor of poorer market opportunities for the small entrepreneur and peasant, the social factor of their loss of social ties and status in the larger society. As the situation of the small entrepreneur continues to deteriorate in the face of the growing rationalization of the economic order, we may expect new mass movements to gain adherents from the old middle classes, and especially their lower sections.

Chapter 12

Isolated Workers

MASS MOVEMENTS mobilize people who are alienated from the going system, who do not believe in the legitimacy of the established order, and who therefore are ready to engage in efforts to destroy it. The greatest number of people available to mass movements will be found in those sections of society that have the fewest ties to the social order, for those who have the fewest opportunities to participate in the formal and informal life of the community have the weakest commitments to existing institutions.

The working classes have the weakest ties to the social order, not only because they receive the smallest benefits from it but also because they have the fewest opportunities to participate in it. Furthermore, the rise of the industrial order has held out the promise to the working classes of full participation in society. As a consequence of the large gap between promise and fulfillment, members of the working classes flock to mass movements in greater proportions than do members of other classes.[21] Furthermore, since the working classes are numerically larger than the other classes, mass movements generally receive their greatest number of followers from this source. This appears to be true of all kinds of mass movements, including Fascist and proto-Fascist move-

---

21. See pp. 180-82, above.

ments as well as Communist and other "left-wing" movements against democratic institutions.

However, as in the instance of the middle classes, the working classes do not respond uniformly to mass movements. It is the workers who are more *isolated* from major channels of communication and institutions that are more available for mobilization by mass movements. This applies both to industrial and farm workers.

Certain industries sharply isolate their workers from the larger society, and therefore these workers are more readily available for mass actions. This may be true even where the workers are *not* isolated from one another, *so long as their organizations are cut off from the society at large.* The isolation of groups as well as of discrete individuals tends to generate feelings of alienation.[22]

The extent to which workers are available in one industry rather than another may be indicated by the frequency of extreme economic and political action, such as violent strikes and support for the Communist party. Reports on Communist strength by industry for seven European countries plus the United States reveal that it is greatest in *coal and metal mining and in maritime and longshore industries* (U. S. Department of State, 1956, pp. 9-21).

The strongest Communist districts in Great Britain have been West Fife, a Scottish mining area, and East Rhondda, a South Wales mining section. A look at the election statistics for these two areas shows the strong support miners have given the Communist party, in sharp contrast to its very weak showing almost everywhere else in Great Britain (see Table 17).

The Communists also have been strong among French and German miners. French coal miners, for example, gave the Communist-controlled C.G.T. its strongest support (Lipset *et al.*, 1954, p. 1138).

22. The following discussion of isolated occupations is indebted to Lipset *et al.* (1954).

TABLE 17.—Communist Vote in Two Mining Areas, Great Britain, 1929-1950.

DATE	West Fife	East Rhondda
1929	15.2%	15.2%
1931	22.1	31.9
1935	37.4*	38.2
1945	42.2*	45.5
1950	21.6	12.7

* Elected.

SOURCE: Pollock et al. (1951, p. 111).

In the United States, the Western Federation of Miners provided over half the membership of the anarcho-syndicalist Industrial Workers of the World at its founding convention in 1905.[23] Following the demise of the I.W.W. after the First World War, the Western Federation of Miners came under Communist control, which persists to this day (the union now is called the Mine, Mill and Smelter Workers' Union, affiliated with the C.I.O. until it was expelled for Communist activities). Together with the sailors and longshoremen, the miners have constituted the major base of the Communists in Australia before World War II.[24] In the United States, too, the maritime and longshore unions have been centers of Communist influence (although the National Maritime Union recently broke with the Communist party). In Canada, the Communist party has obtained major support from miners and seamen. In Scandinavia, also, there is evidence of extremist support among sailors and longshoremen, as well as miners (Lipset et al., 1954, pp. 1137-8).[25]

A study of the propensity to strike by industry for eleven countries (five of which are included in the reports on com-

---

23. Twenty-seven thousand out of fifty thousand members of the I.W.W. came from the Western Federation of Miners (Brissenden, 1920, p. 74).

24. See Overacker (1952, pp. 116-33, 165, 180-90).

25. The role of miners in mass movements evidently is not new, since Thomas Muntzer is said to have relied "above all . . . on the workers in the copper-mines at Mansfeld" for the hard core of the millennial movement which he led in the sixteenth century (Cohn, 1957, p. 266)

munist strength, cited above) shows that strikes, also, are the most frequent in the mining and maritime industries (Kerr and Siegel, 1954, p. 190). Furthermore, the quality of the strikes in these industries is marked by greater violence and an element of revolt, rather than by bargaining tactics for limited economic aims alone. For example, two of the greatest general strikes of recent times developed out of the English coal mines and the American waterfront; and many other general strikes evolved from disputes in the mines or on the waterfront (as in England in 1842, France in 1902 and 1904, Holland in 1903, Italy in 1903).

The propensity to engage in violent strikes and the propensity to support the Communists probably are not so much reciprocally determining as they are similarly determined by the social structure of the affected industries. These industries were subject to many strikes before the Communists became active, "but their efforts certainly have served to intensify the conflict in these already favorable environments" (Kerr and Siegel, 1954, p. 201). What requires explanation is the fact that the *same* industries in many different countries are associated with marked tendencies toward mass actions.

Mining, maritime, and longshore industries have this in common: their workers form a largely undifferentiated and socially isolated mass. "Some of these communities, such as the coal towns, are geographically isolated, while others, such as waterfront districts, are socially isolated within metropolitan communities." There are few autonomous or neutral structures in them "to mediate the conflicts and dilute the mass." They have little occupational stratification, nor do they have

. . . the myriad of voluntary associations with mixed memberships which characterize the multi-industry town. The force of public opinion must seem rather weak to the . . . miner in the coal patch who never sees "the public." . . . The employer . . . is usually an absentee owner who . . . exhausts a mine and moves on or hires longshoremen on a casual basis or gets his views of personnel relations from the law on mutiny. The worker is as detached from the employer as from the community at large. (Kerr and Siegel, 1954, pp. 191-2)

At the same time, these workers live in their own separate communities: the ship, the waterfront, the coal town. Hence they have fairly continuous contact with one another, especially since it is hard for them to move to another community or to move into a higher job. As a result of this density of internal contacts, combined with the paucity of external relations, common grievances readily emerge and become shared rather than dispersed. For they are held at the same time, at the same place, and against the same people, and they are therefore easily spread and easily transformed into collective symbols. These "mass grievances," not the individual disgruntlement, are the sources of collective violence and mass movements in these industries (Kerr and Siegel, 1954, pp. 191-2).

Communist strength among lumbermen also might be accounted for in terms of the "isolated mass." Norwegian lumbermen manifest a strong propensity toward the Communist party, as well as a strong tendency to strike. Lumbering areas in Sweden, too, give the Communists a higher vote than do even the large industrial areas. The prominence of lumbermen in the old I.W.W. also indicates their tendency toward extremism. Another industry which possesses the characteristics of a group apart is the fishing industry; and around the world, commercial fishermen tend toward extremism relative to workers in other industries. For example, the fishermen of Iceland support the strongest Communist party in Scandinavia. And in the United States the west-coast fishermen are traditionally militant and are organized in a Communist-dominated union, even though they are mostly owners or part-owners of their own boats. Finally, the above average tendency of metal workers to engage in extremist activities, as in Germany, in part may be accounted for in these same terms. However, the much greater occupational stratification in metal mining, which separates workers from one another and creates a ladder of jobs for individual mobility, may help account for the fact that these tendencies are not more marked in isolated towns given over to this industry.[26]

In contrast to these isolated industries, whose workers are given to extremism, the lack of strikes and the absence of Communist support in, for example, trade and service industries, may be explained in terms of relatively higher levels of integration into the larger society. Workers in the latter industries are more likely "to live in multi-industry communities, to associate with people with quite different working experiences than their own, and to belong to associations with heterogeneous memberships." In consequence, their behavior is sharply different from those isolated masses "more or less permanently at odds with the community at large" (Kerr and Siegel, 1954, p. 193).

It remains to be clarified how workers living in cohesive communities of their own may be described as "isolated." Obviously, miners, for example, are not isolated from each other, but on the contrary are in continuous social interaction. The distinction made earlier between individual and group isolation is pertinent here. Mining communities, though they protect workers from personal isolation, do not relate them to the outside world. The miner is isolated and *feels isolated* from centers of power and activity in the society at large—relative to workers located in centers of communication and transportation.

Thus, many of those districts in Sweden with a relatively heavy Communist vote are geographically isolated, without individual members being isolated from one another. People living in such areas are usually the last to receive schools, churches, railroads and telephone service. They feel they are

---

26. See Lipset *et al.* (1954, pp. 1137-8) ; and Kerr and Siegel (1954, p. 192) .

being neglected, and develop a "collective inferiority complex" which is reinforced by the tendency of people in other areas to look down on the "backward" communities. As a result, there develops "a climate of resentment against the larger society—a climate in which communism can thrive."

For example, some foreign minorities in Sweden tend to vote Communist, while others do not. The evidence suggests that those minorities which are respected by the Swedish population (e.g., the mountain Lapps) tend to support the non-Communist parties, while those which are socially isolated (e.g., the forest Lapps) tend to vote Communist. (Davison, 1954-55, p. 378)

Finally, it may be noted once again that the "kind of social isolation that is associated with Communist voting behavior [in Sweden] is ordinarily not caused by individual maladjustment. Those who vote Communist usually seem to have satisfactory primary group relations in the home, factory, and community" (Davison, 1954-55, p. 378). Isolated communities are analagous to *isolated primary groups*, which, as we have pointed out earlier, are not capable of linking the individual and the society.

Furthermore, the combination of internal contact and external isolation facilitates the work of the mass agitator. In the absence of internal communication between the people he wants to mobilize, the agitator must reach each person individually, and cannot depend on other persons to help solidify the individual's favorable response to his appeal. This communication problem for the agitator is one of the major reasons why the vulnerability of large numbers to mass appeals often does not get translated into mass action. Where people are massed together but possess few relations to the larger society, there is the best opportunity for the mobilizer of mass movements. This is the condition of, for example, longshoremen, as against a highly dispersed population such as farm laborers.

Farm laborers are practically without stable organization or social relations of any kind. If this makes them more available for mobilization, it also makes them hard to reach. That is to say, farm laborers possess few resistances to mass movements, but the very isolation which makes them so disposed makes them less likely to be contacted by such movements. Their extreme geographical mobility also prevents easy organization. Therefore, action on their part, when it does occur, often is confined to sporadic strikes. Nevertheless, much of the I.W.W. membership was composed of migratory farm workers (McWilliams, 1939, p. 155). The previously unorganized farm laborers of Italy made up 26% of the Fascist party in 1921 (Finer, 1935, p. 143). Fifty per cent of Italian farm laborers expressed a preference for the Communist party in 1953 (*Italian Political Party Preferences,* 1953). In Germany, nazism took root more easily in areas where class consciousness and organization among rural laborers was still in its infancy, than in areas where labor had been organized politically and in unions for considerable time (Heberle, 1951, p. 233). Although "traditionally, no political movement has ever succeeded in gaining the solid sympathies of [French] rural labor" (Ehrmann, 1952, p. 39), its extremist responses are frequent. Probably mass tendencies are maximized when rural laborers become concentrated in large numbers, especially when they live apart from the landowners in isolated villages. Extremist responses are minimized when rural laborers work one to a farm and live with the farm family (Lipset and Linz, 1956, chap. xii).

Although workers who support totalitarian movements are more likely to favor communism than fascism, it should be recalled that workers also have given support to Fascist movements. Thus, 42% of the Nazi party membership in 1933 was made up of manual and service workers, not too much less than their proportion in the labor force—52% (Gerth, 1952, p. 106). In the Italian Fascist party in 1922, one finds a comparable proportion of workers, 43½% of the membership falling into this category (Finer, 1935, p. 143). Class theory finds such data to be highly deviant, since these movements opposed working-class organizations, including especially working-class political parties. Mass theory, on the other hand, expects Fascist movements as well as Communist movements to gain a large following among workers, since according to this theory people do not support Fascists or Communists primarily to further their economic interests, but as an expression of their resentment and hostility against the established order and in response to the pseudo-authority and pseudo-community provided by the totalitarian movement.

In summary, workers who are socially isolated manifest the greater susceptibility to mass tendencies. This is reflected in the greater extremism of workers in mining and maritime industries, since these industries isolate their workers from the larger society. It also is reflected in the extremism of workers who are isolated by prolonged unemployment, as we have shown in Part II. Finally, it is reflected in differences between skilled and unskilled workers: unskilled workers generally possess the weaker social ties,[27] and for this reason (along with their lack of education) they have the weaker commitment to democratic values. Tables 18, 19, and 20 show that among German, French, and Italian workers, those who have the higher-skilled and better-paid jobs are more likely to express preference for democratic institutions and parties.

The evidence which has been analyzed in Part III supports the view that it is the more isolated members of all social classes who gravitate toward mass movements. People who have few ties to the existing order are available for political adventures against that order. The individual's vulnerability to mass movements is not determined by economic

---

27. For data on the relative lack of libertarianism and social ties among unskilled and low-income workers, compared with skilled and high-income workers, see Tables 5 and 6, pp. 69-72, above. There appear to be some exceptions to the generalization that unskilled workers support extremist movements more strongly than do skilled workers. Sweden is one of these cases (Davison, 1954-55, p. 384) .

TABLE 18.—Party System Desired by German Workers, by Level of Skill, 1953.

	PER CENT DESIRING		
LEVEL OF SKILL	Several Parties	One or No Party	No Opinion
Skilled	65	27	8
Semiskilled	49	35	16
Unskilled	40	38	22

SOURCE: Lipset (n.d., p. 4).

TABLE 19.—Preference of French Male Industrial Workers for Socialist and Communist Parties, by Economic Level, 1954.

	PER CENT OF ESTIMATED NUMBER OF VOTERS PREFERRING	
ECONOMIC LEVEL	Socialists	Communists
Above average	34	15
Average	22	32
Poor	17	34

SOURCE: Data recomputed from Stoetzel (1955, p. 118).

TABLE 20.—Preference of Italian Workers for Socialist and Communist Parties, by Economic Level, 1953.

	PER CENT PREFERRING		
ECONOMIC LEVEL	Right Socialists	Left Socialists	Communists
Average	10	17	17
Below average	10	28	31
Poor	3	18	54

SOURCE: Recomputation by S. M. Lipset of data from "Italian Political Party Preferences" (1953, p. 12). Left Socialists were in coalition with the Communists.

interests alone; the crucial question is whether the individual has attachments to occupation, association, and community. The reality of democratic values and institutional rules either impinges on him through these affiliations, or not in any firm way.

The general argument of Part III has been well-stated by a French political sociologist in these words:

Millenarianism spreads only in societies in which individuals in great numbers are "available," or in other words consent to break with the existing state of things and place their hopes in an order to be created instead of in the established order. This availability is not necessarily the measure of the real evils of the society; many stable societies have revealed greater injustice, on subsequent examination, than societies shaken by revolutionary disorders. It is the measure of the *judgments* men form of the society in which they live, or rather of the feelings that they hold toward their immediate environment. The French worker's lot has certainly improved since 1850 or since 1900. Nevertheless he is more rebellious in 1950 than he was fifty or a hundred years ago, more convinced that he is a victim of permanent injustice, and also that he can expect nothing from progress within the so-called capitalist world. In other words, the tendency toward millenarianism is connected above all with the idea or the feeling expressed in the everyday phrase, "You can't expect anything from those people," or "You can't expect anything from this world." The deciding factor is not that men criticize or even that they detest the rich, the masters, the state; the essential thing is that they despair of everything known, and that they hope for everything from a glowing and unknown future. If such is the essence of millenarianism, it is understandable that it can seduce common men as well as intellectuals, Chinese peasants as well as Renault workers; *their common characteristic is the phenomenon of breaking with what is* just as much as the phenomenon of faith in what will be. (Aron, 1953, pp. 8-9; italics added)

Summary of Part III

1. Mass movements recruit people from all major social strata.

a) Fascist movements that gain a large following mobilize many members of the working classes as well as the middle classes.

b) Communist movements are more class-homogeneous than Fascist movements, but they also attract people from all classes.

2. Lower social strata are more responsive to mass appeals than are higher strata. However, *within all strata,* those with the fewest social ties are the most receptive to mass appeals. The first-named social category in each of the following pairs possesses the fewer social ties and is the more responsive to mass movements:

a) free-lance intellectuals vs. intellectuals in corporate bodies (e.g., universities);

b) new business vs. old business;

c) small business vs. big business;

d) unskilled workers vs. skilled workers;

e) mining and maritime workers vs. workers in other kinds of industry;

f) poorer farmers and farm laborers vs. wealthier farmers;

g) youth (especially students) vs. adults;

h) politically apathetic vs. politically involved;

i) unemployed vs. employed.

CONCLUSION

Chapter 13

Mass Society and
Democratic Order

THE PRESENT study has examined conditions in Western society that favor mass politics. Mass politics occurs when large numbers of people engage in political activity outside of the procedures and rules instituted by a society to govern political action. Mass politics in democratic society therefore is anti-democratic, since it contravenes the constitutional order. The extreme case of mass politics is the totalitarian movement, notably communism and fascism. Less extreme examples of mass politics are McCarthyism and Poujadism.

Modern democratic systems possess a distinct vulnerability to mass politics because they invite the whole population, most of which has historically been politically quiescent, to engage in politics. However, this does not mean that all or even most democratic systems succumb to mass politics. The problem is to identify those factors that increase the vulnerability of democratic systems to mass politics, and those that decrease it, in order to be able to specify the conditions that may strengthen democratic politics and civil liberty.

The most satisfactory theory of the vulnerability of social systems to mass politics is the theory of mass society. This theory has two major versions. One, which may be called the aristocratic criticism, asserts that the primary cause of mass politics lies in the loss of exclusiveness of elites as a result of the rise of popular participation in the critical centers of society. According to this version of the theory of mass society, the main danger to political order and civil liberty is the domination of elites by masses. The other version, which may be called the democratic criticism, stresses the vulnerability of masses to domination by elites. This danger to political order and civil liberty is believed to result from the atomization of society and the rise of elites capable of mobilizing isolated and unattached people. A combination of these two versions produces a stronger theory than either one alone. This integrated theory of mass society locates the causes of mass politics in the condition of both elites and non-elites, that is, in the total social structure and especially in the structure of groups intermediate between the state and the family.

"Mass society," then, is treated as an abstract type. It is always a question of the *degree* to which an actual society is a "mass society." A society is a "mass society" to the extent that both elites and non-elites are directly accessible to one another by virtue of the weakness of groups capable of mediating between them. Insofar as these conditions prevail, neither elites nor non-elites are capable of preventing frequent political activity outside of established channels. Other types of society are more capable of minimizing mass politics (and other forms of mass behavior). Since both elites and non-elites are bound by fixed status in communal (e.g., feudal) society, there is little mass behavior in this kind of system. Since non-elites are bound by multiple group affiliations of their own choosing in pluralist (e.g., liberal) society, there is relatively little mass politics in this kind of system. Since non-elites are subject to extensive control by the political elite in totalitarian (e.g., Communist and Fascist) society, there is little mass politics in this kind of system.

By means of this theory of mass society, a large number of observations on political phenomena in particular organizations, classes, communities, and whole societies can be fitted together to form a coherent picture of the conditions that favor mass behavior in politics. Groups which are particularly vulnerable to mass movements manifest major discontinuities in their structure during periods of change. Thus, communism and fascism have gained strength in social systems undergoing sudden and extensive changes in the structure of authority and community. Sharp tears in the social fabric caused by widespread unemployment or by major military defeat are highly favorable to mass politics. Social classes which provide disproportionate support for mass movements are those that possess the fewest social ties among their members. This means above all the lower social classes. However, since there are sections of all social classes which tend to be socially atomized, members of all social classes are to be found among the participants in mass politics: unattached (especially free-lance) intellectuals, marginal (especially small) businessmen and farmers, and isolated workers have engaged in mass politics in times of crisis.

In the preceding pages, we have stated conditions which favor mass movements destructive of political order and civil liberty. We now shall summarize our analysis by assessing what it implies about the conditions favorable to liberal democracy. This should help to dispel fears that a theory of mass society necessarily is antagonistic to liberal democratic values, or that it is a prophecy of doom.

The theory of mass society stresses the need for the autonomy of certain social units if order with freedom is to be secured. The various versions of this theory tend to divide into two camps according to whether primary stress is placed on the autonomy of elites or on the autonomy of non-elites. The aristocratic view stresses the need for the independence of elites on the premise that constitutional liberty above all requires leadership with the capacity to define, exemplify, and defend it. The democratic view stresses the need for the independence of non-elites on the premise that constitutional liberty above all requires safeguards against the accumulation of power by any group, especially elites. In this fundamental matter, the two views are not incompatible; on the contrary, each is strengthened when it is combined with the other. Civil liberty requires considerable social autonomy of *both* elites and non-elites. This means specifically that elites and non-elites must have the following characteristics:

(a) There must be extensive self-government, private as well as public, and individuals must belong to several self-governing units.

(b) There must be extensive opportunities for elites to formulate policies and take action without *ad hoc* interference from the outside.

However, democracy entails a fundamental restriction on the autonomy of elites, especially in politics. This restriction is twofold: first, elites will be restricted by one another in that they will be constrained to compete with one another for leadership; and secondly, elites will be restricted by non-elites in that they will be constrained to compete for the people's votes. An implication of this conception of democracy also involves a restriction on non-elites: the electorate will accept the leadership that they have selected, until the time when it may be rejected according to duly constituted procedure.[1]

In summary, a liberal democracy requires widespread participation in the selection of leaders, and a large amount of self-governing activity on the part of non-elites. It also requires competition among leaders and would-be leaders, and considerable autonomy for those who win positions of leadership. The basic question arises, what kind of social structure will meet these conditions of liberal democracy? The theory of mass society expounded in the present study implies that social pluralism is a social arrangement which performs this function. A plurality of independent and limited-function groups supports liberal democracy by providing social bases of free and open competition for leadership, widespread participation in the selection of leaders, restraint

---

1. See Schumpeter (1947, pp. 269-96).

in the application of pressures on leaders, and self-government in wide areas of social life. Therefore, where social pluralism is strong, liberty and democracy tend to be strong; and conversely, forces which weaken social pluralism also weaken liberty and democracy.

In the transition from medieval to modern society, the extent to which pluralist forms emerged as substitutes for communal forms was one decisive factor which determined the fate of liberal democracy. Social pluralism flourished in Northwestern Europe and in North America, and these are the areas where liberty and democracy have found their greatest strength. In seventeenth century England, for example, a plurality of class and religious groups already were developing strong roots. As a consequence, it was possible for new social forms adapted to the requirements of urban-industrial life to emerge from older relations. For a long time, it has been widely feared that urban-industrial conditions would destroy an independent group life. But in the modern world, it is among the highly urbanized and industrialized societies that social pluralism and liberal democracy have achieved their fullest and firmest expression. The Communist movement, for example, has won its widest following within the less industrialized societies of the Western world—in Italy and France,[2] rather than in such nations as Britain or the United States. Liberal democracy is strongest in countries possessing the highest per capita output of industrial energy and personal income (for example, among Western countries, the correlation between size of Communist vote and per capita energy is —.83; and the correlation between size of Communist vote and per capita income is —.93).[3]

But the fact that countries like the Soviet Union are attaining high levels of economic development without liberty or democracy shows that the extent of industrialization alone

2. However, France is now undergoing a rapid industrial expansion.
3. On the sources of data, see pp. 150 (n. 20), 160 (n. 28).

is not decisive. More important is the mode of economic development, especially whether that development is accomplished through pluralist as well as bureaucratic agencies. Where economic development takes place by means of a variety of social forms, including private as well as public enterprises, liberty and democracy are more likely to grow than where it occurs under the exclusive aegis of the state.

In any case, Marx was wrong: it is not the most highly developed capitalist systems which reveal the greatest social unrest and revolutionary tendencies. Instead, this has been the fate of the less developed countries of Europe (and, even more, of Asia and Africa).

But if Marx is wrong, will Weber prove to be right? For Weber, bureaucratization, not the class struggle, provides the central dynamic of the modern world (1946, p. 49). It is widely believed that bureaucracy constitutes the strongest threat to social pluralism and liberal democracy in the highly industrialized countries. This view raises important issues about the future development of American society. Several of these issues are briefly noted in the remaining pages.

One of the most prominent arguments which attribute mass consequences to the rationalization of organization focuses on the transformation of the middle classes: the advent of large corporate organization at the expense of small productive property transforms the bases of middle-class power and undermines the capacity of this class to continue as a major pluralist force in the contemporary social order (Mills, 1956, p. 262). If an independent middle class served to support democratic rule prior to the emergence of large-scale urban-industrial organization, it is believed that the ascendancy of bureaucratic organization now threatens to atomize the middle classes and as a result weaken the social foundations of liberal democracy. The shift from the old to the new middle classes is fraught with peril, according to this line of reasoning.

The trouble with this argument is that it is based on too

narrow a conception of the bases of social participation and social power. It may be granted that the property basis of social power and participation is weakened by the shift from an entrepeneurial to an employee society. But at the same time new forms of organization, such as professional associations and civic groups, have been developing to take its place. As a result, members of the new middle class have high rates of participation in voluntary associations, political affairs, and community life.

A burgeoning literature of social criticism is directed toward the meaning of this heightened participation of the new middle classes, especially in the United States. Some social critics of the new middle class argue that far from being non-participants, members of this class engage in group activity to such an extent that they lose their autonomy as individuals. This is the major characteristic imputed to the "organization man," who is absorbed by the organization for which he works and whose family is absorbed by the (suburban) community in which he lives.[4] The threat to individual autonomy is believed to lie not in the lack of organization but in the inclusiveness of relations to the organization: the hold of the modern corporation over its members begins to resemble that of the medieval corporation over its members. A closely related issue concerns the quality of many community,[5] religious,[6] and other social ties of members of this class: these relations are often alleged to mask an underlying passivity and lack of commitment, and to feed on a widespread disposition to overconform. These issues remain to be settled, but in any case, the evidence does not support the contention that the new middle classes are composed of atomized masses.

A second prominent argument that attributes mass consequences to the ascendancy of large-scale organization focuses

---

4. See Whyte (1957).
5. See Whyte (1957, Part VII).
6. See Herberg (1955).

on the transformation of the public realm. It is frequently asserted that the expanding scale of bureaucratic organization tends to *centralize* public activities and to substitute administration for politics, and therefore to undermine the basis for political participation. But if many people feel ineffective in public affairs, it is in no small part due to the complexity of public problems and events, rather than the result of the lack of opportunity to engage in political activities. In many ways, national politics are more accessible than they have been in the past (although the secrecy surrounding matters of national security is a major force decreasing access). But the growing scope and complexity of the public realm have made distant decisions and events more decisive for private life and simultaneously less manageable. The local community is less and less the locus of major decisions, so that local self-government cannot have the same significance today that it once did. However, it continues to play an important role in some spheres, for example, in public education in the United States.

Commensurate with the nationalization and even internationalization of the public realm is the comparable shift in the locus of communication. The major media of communication tend to be highly sensitive to their audiences (witness the spread of public opinion polls, market research, etc.). They seek to reflect as well as shape nation-wide opinion, and thereby increase its influence on national policies. Thus there arises the paradox of high *aggregate* access combined with low *individual* access—so that the individual who is responding as an individual feels isolated, and participates psychologically in the power of the aggregate only to the extent that he (along with his personal associates) is capable of identifying himself with his anonymous fellows.

A feeling of political impotence does not stem from the powerlessness of the individual alone. When, after all, have most individuals *qua* individuals been able to readily affect the outcome of public issues? The sense of ineffectiveness results also from the difficulty for citizens to meet and speak together in a public realm dominated by issues of great complexity and by impersonal means of communication. Political apathy would appear to be in large part a response to the resulting distance between the citizen and the locus of major events. However, there are important differences among subgroups in the degree of political apathy and powerlessness. Certain kinds of people, by virtue of their training and position in society, are in relatively better positions to hear and be heard as individuals. This is especially true for professional leaders in government, in business, and, to a lesser extent, in labor—men who are believed to be and consider themselves qualified to head up major institutions by virtue of their education and training. It is also true for the rapidly increasing proportion of the population that is receiving a higher education and going into professional occupations.

Closely related to the question of the impact of large-scale organization on participation in politics is the issue of its consequences for pluralist authority. There are those who believe that American elites are becoming increasingly responsive, even hypersensitive, to public demands and to one another, so much so that leadership and authority are seriously weakened. Thus Lippmann (1956) is concerned that the great complexities and needs of foreign policy in the nuclear age are being denied by virtue of public pressures on foreign-policy makers. There are those, on the other hand, who believe that American elites increasingly constitute a closed and unified group, so much so that liberty and democracy are seriously weakened. Thus Mills (1956) is concerned that the great consequences of foreign policy are being suffered by a public which has little hand in their determination.

The present study has sought to show that directly accessible elites make ready targets for mass movements. Constitutions and other appropriate institutional devices are needed to regulate access to elites, and to reduce pressures on them (Schumpeter, 1947, p. 288). But this does not mean that the mere insulation of elites protects liberty and democracy. Ultimate control over elites must be lodged in the community, even as elites are needed to set specific standards and to propose and implement detailed policies. If democratic institutions are to remain salient, even the complex and perilous nature of international relations cannot justify the abrogation of free competition for national leadership. But is it true that the main drift is toward a closed and unified elite? Such a view cannot account for the increasing social representativeness of national elites, nor for the myriad of conflicts among them, and still less can it be made consistent with the growth of powerful organizations among previously unorganized segments of the community (for example, among industrial workers and among Negroes in the United States).

Furthermore, the power of government cannot be viewed merely defensively, as a danger to the community which therefore must take all precautions to limit it. Power also is the capacity to achieve goals, and therefore must be granted to and assumed by those who possess special competence to use it. The very concept of elite is distasteful to many democrats, so much so that those who are elite often feel illegitimate and those who are not elite feel resentful. Herein lies a fundamental dilemma for democracy, the adaptation to which requires widespread appreciation of *the necessary tension between elites and non-elites.*

The major guarantee against the aggrandizement of power by elites is the existence of a plurality of groups that are equal enough in power to generate genuine competition for leadership on the several levels of political society. A danger of bureaucratization is that it will undermine the bases for a plurality of group interests and organizations. For example, it may undermine class organization, so that people in a similar class situation, who therefore have certain economic interests in common, will despair of improving those interests through joint action, and consequently attach themselves to mass movements subversive of all groups, including classes. The nihilism of masses tends to be a greater threat to liberal democracy than the antagonism between classes. Actions taken for economic interests tend to be moderate; whereas mass actions tend to be extremist. A good part of the response to mass appeals is an expression of social atomization, rather than action oriented toward either self interest or the public interest. *Differences in receptivity to mass symbols and leaders are due primarily to the strength of social ties, and not to the influence of class, or any other social status, by itself.*

The central problem posed by the theory of mass society is that of *social alienation,* or the distance between the individual and his society. Social alienation may occur on all levels of society. The mark of mass society is the alienation of elites as well as the alienation of non-elites. Social alienation has increased with the dissolution of medieval society. Aristocratic critics of mass tendencies offer no solution when they beckon us back to a society based on status: certain social processes are irreversible, and among them is the growing equality of condition. Democratic critics of mass society also do not consider alternative outcomes of the modernization of the world when they assert that urbanization and industrialization, and the correlative spread of large-scale organization entail alienation; for in this case, too, we are confronted with irreversible social processes. The present study has sought to argue that these conditions of modern life carry with them both the heightened possibility of social alienation *and* enhanced opportunities for the creation of new forms of association. Modern industry destroys the conditions for a society of small enterprises, but it also provides the condition of abundance which frees people to seek new ways of life. Modern urban life atomizes traditional social groups, but it also provides a variety of contacts and experiences that broaden social horizons and the range of social participation. Modern democracy diminishes the legitimacy of elites, but it also encourages a multiplicity of competing elites. By enlarging our understanding of such diverse potentialities in the modern world, concepts of mass society and social pluralism promise to stimulate further studies of the social bases of political integration and autonomy.

References

ADORNO, T. W. *et al. The Authoritarian Personality.* New York: Harper and Bros., 1950.

ALMOND, GABRIEL A. *The Appeals of Communism.* Princeton: Princeton University Press, 1954.

ALMOND, GABRIEL A. "The Politics of German Business," in *West German Leadership and Foreign Policy,* ed. HANS SPEIER and W. PHILLIPS DAVISON, pp. 195-241. Evanston: Row, Peterson, 1957.

AMIS, KINGSLEY. *Socialism and the Intellectuals.* London: The Fabian Society, 1957.

ANDERSON, EVELYN. *Hammer or Anvil: The Story of the German Working-Class Movement.* London: Victor Gollancz, 1945.

ARENDT, HANNAH. *The Origins of Totalitarianism.* New York: Harcourt, Brace, 1951.

ARENDT, HANNAH. "Authority in the Twentieth Century," *The Review of Politics,* XVIII (1956), 403-17.

ARENDT, HANNAH. *The Human Condition.* Chicago: University of Chicago Press, 1958.

ARON, RAYMOND. "Totalitarianism and Freedom," *Confluence,* II (June, 1953), 3-20.

AXELROD, MORRIS. "Urban Structure and Social Participation," *American Sociological Review,* XXI (1956), 13-18.

BABBITT, IRVING. *Democracy and Leadership.* Boston: Houghton Mifflin, 1924.

BAKKE, E. WIGHT. *Citizens Without Work.* New Haven: Yale University Press, 1940.

BECKER, HOWARD. *German Youth: Bond or Free.* New York: Oxford University Press, 1946.

BELL, DANIEL. "The Background and Development of Marxian Socialism in the United States," in *Socialism and American Life,* Vol. I, ed. DONALD EGBERT and STOW PERSONS, pp. 213-405. Princeton: Princeton University Press, 1952.

BELL, DANIEL. "The Theory of Mass Society, A Critique," *Commentary,* XXXII (July, 1956), 75-83.

BENDIX, REINHARD. "Social Stratification and Political Power," *American Political Science Review,* XLVI (1952), 357-75.

BENDIX, REINHARD. *Work and Authority in Industry.* New York: John Wiley and Sons, 1956.

BETTELHEIM, BRUNO. "Individual Autonomy and Mass Controls," in *Sociologica: Aufsätze Max Horkheimer,* ed. THEODOR W. ADORNO and WALTER DIRKS, pp. 245-62. Frankfurt Am Main: Europaische Verlaganstalt, 1955.

BLUMER, HERBERT. "Collective Behavior," in *New Outlines of the Principles of Sociology,* ed. A. M. LEE, pp. 165-222. New York: Barnes and Noble, 1946.

BONHAM, JOHN. *The Middle Class Vote.* London: Faber and Faber, 1954.

BORGESE, G. A. *Goliath, the March of Fascism.* New York: Viking Press, 1937.

BORKENAU, FRANZ. *The Communist International.* London: Faber and Faber, 1938.

BRACKER, KARL. *Die Auflosung der Weimarer Republik.* Stuttgart: Ring Verlag, 1955.

BRINTON, CRANE. *The Anatomy of Revolution.* New York: Prentice-Hall, 1952.

BRISSENDEN, PAUL F. *The I.W.W.: A Study of American Syndicalism.* New York: Columbia University Press, 1920.

BRUTZKUS, BORIS. "The Historical Peculiarities of the Social and Economic Development of Russia," in *Class, Status and Power,* ed. REINHARD BENDIX and S. M. LIPSET, pp. 517-40. Glencoe: The Free Press, 1953.

BRZEZINSKI, ZBIGNIEUO K. *The Permanent Purge.* Cambridge: Harvard University Press, 1955.

BULLOCK, ALAN. *Hitler: A Study in Tyranny.* London: Odhams Press, 1952.

BURCKHARDT, JACOB. *Force and Freedom.* New York: Meridian Books, 1955.

CAMPBELL, ANGUS; GURIN, G.; and MILLER, W. *The Voter Decides.* Evanston: Row, Peterson, 1954.

CANTRIL, HADLEY (ed.). *Public Opinion 1935-1946.* Princeton: Princeton University Press, 1951.

CANTRIL, HADLEY. *The Politics of Despair.* New York: Basic Books, 1958.

CHAMBERLIN, WILLIAM H. *The Russian Revolution.* New York: Macmillan, 1935.

COHN, NORMAN. *The Pursuit of the Millennium.* Fairlawn: Essential Books, 1957.

COLE, G. D. H. *A History of the Labour Party from 1914.* London: Routledge and Kegan Paul, 1948.

COLEMAN, JAMES S. *Community Conflict.* Glencoe: The Free Press, 1957.

COSER, LEWIS. "But on Other Terms . . .," *Dissent*, I (Summer, 1954), 234-41.

CROSSMAN, RICHARD (ed.). *The God that Failed.* New York: Harper and Bros., 1949.

DAHL, ROBERT. *A Preface to Democratic Theory.* Chicago: University of Chicago Press, 1956.

DAVISON, W. PHILLIPS. "A Review of Sven Rydenfell's *Communism in Sweden,*" *Public Opinion Quarterly*, XVIII (1954-55), 375-88.

DEGRÉ, GERARD. "Freedom and Social Structure," *American Sociological Review*, XI (1946), 529-36.

DITTMANN, WILHELM. *Das Politische Deutschland vor Hitler.* Zurich: Europa Verlag A. G., 1945.

DOERNE, MARTIN. "Problems of the German University," in *The University in a Changing World*, ed. W. M. KOTSCHNIG and E. PRYS, pp. 53-84. London: Oxford University Press, 1932.

DURKHEIM, EMILE. *Suicide.* Glencoe: The Free Press, 1951.

DURKHEIM, EMILE. *Professional Ethics and Civic Morals.* Glencoe: The Free Press, 1958.

DYNES, RUSSELL R. "Church-Sect Typology and Socio-Economic Status," *American Sociological Review*, XX (1955), 555-60.

EBENSTEIN, WILLIAM. *Fascist Italy.* New York: American Book Co., 1939.

EBENSTEIN, WILLIAM. *Today's Isms.* New York: Prentice-Hall, 1954.

EHRMANN, HENRY. "The French Peasant and Communism," *American Political Science Review*, IV (1952), 19-43.

EINAUDI, MARIO; DOMENACH, J.; and GAROSCHI, A. *Communism in Western Europe.* Ithaca: Cornell University Press, 1951.

EISENBERG, PHILIP, and LAZARSFELD, PAUL. "The Psychological Effect of Unemployment," *Psychological Bulletin*, XXXV (1938), 358-90.

ELIOT, T. S. *Notes Towards the Definition of Culture.* London: Faber and Faber, 1948.

FAINSOD, MERLE. *How Russia Is Ruled.* Cambridge: Harvard University Press, 1953.

"The Federalist No. 51," in *The Federalist*, pp. 335-41. New York: Random House, 1941.

FIEDLER, LESLIE. "The Middle Against Both Ends," *Encounter*, V (August, 1955), 16-23.

FINER, HERMAN. *Mussolini's Italy.* London: Victor Gollancz Ltd., 1935.

FINER, HERMAN. *Theory and Practice of Modern Government.* New York: Henry Holt, 1949.

FLORINSKY, MICHAEL T. *The End of the Russian Empire.* New Haven: Yale University Press, 1931.

FOSKETT, JOHN M. "Social Structure and Social Participation," *American Sociological Review*, XX (1955), 431-38.

FRIEDRICH, CARL J. "The Agricultural Basis of Emotional Nationalism," *Public Opinion Quarterly*, VI (1937), 50-61.

FRIEDRICH, CARL J. "The Unique Character of Totalitarian Society," in *Totalitarianism*, ed. CARL J. FRIEDRICH, pp. 47-60. Cambridge: Harvard University Press, 1954.

FROMM, ERICH. *Escape from Freedom*. New York: Farrar and Rinehart, 1941.

FROMM, ERICH. *The Sane Society*. New York: Rinehart, 1955.

GALENSON, WALTER. "Scandinavia," in *Comparative Labor Movements*, ed. WALTER GALENSON, pp. 104-72. New York: Prentice-Hall, 1952.

GALENSON, WALTER, and ZELLNER, ARNOLD. "International Comparisons of Unemployment Rates," in *The Measurement and Behavior of Unemployment*, A Report of the NATIONAL BUREAU OF ECONOMIC RESEARCH, pp. 439-583. Princeton: Princeton University Press, 1957.

GALLAGHER, ORVELL R. "Voluntary Associations in France," *Social Forces*, XXXVI (1957), 153-60.

GAY, PETER. *The Dilemma of Democratic Socialism*. New York: Columbia University Press, 1952.

GEIGER, THEODOR. *Aufgaben und Stellung der Intelligenz in der Gesellschaft*. Stuttgart: Ferdinand Enke Verlag, 1949.

GERMANI, GINO. *Integracion Politica de las Mesasyel Totalitarismo*. Buenos Aires: Colegio Libre De Estudios Superiores, 1956.

GERTH, HANS H. "The Nazi Party: Its Leadership and Composition," in *Reader in Bureaucracy*, ed. ROBERT K. MERTON et al., pp. 100-113. Glencoe: The Free Press, 1952.

GREER, SCOTT. "Individual Participation in Mass Society," in *Approaches to the Study of Politics*, ed. ROLAND YOUNG, pp. 329-42. Evanston: Northwestern University Press, 1958.

GRODZINS, MORTON. *The Loyal and the Disloyal*. Chicago: University of Chicago Press, 1956.

HALLGARTEN, GEORGE W. F. "Adolph Hitler and German Heavy Industry, 1931-1933," *The Journal of Economic History*, XII (1952), 222-46.

HARTZ, LOUIS. *The Liberal Tradition in America*. New York: Harcourt, Brace, 1955.

HASTINGS, PHILIP K. "The Non-Voter in 1952: A Study of Pittsfield, Massachusetts," *Journal of Psychology*, XXXVIII (1954), 301-12.

HASTINGS, PHILIP K. "The Voter and the Non-Voter," *The American Journal of Sociology*, LXII (1956), 302-7.

HEBERLE, RUDOLF. *From Democracy to Nazism*. Baton Rouge: Louisiana State University Press, 1945.

HEBERLE, RUDOLF. *Social Movements*. New York: Appleton-Century-Crofts, 1951.

HEBERLE, RUDOLF, and BERTRAND, A. "Factors Motivating Voting Behavior in a One-Party State," *Social Forces*, XXVII (1949), 343-50.

HEIDEN, KONRAD. *Der Fuehrer, Hitler's Rise to Power*. Boston: Houghton Mifflin, 1944.

HERBERG, WILL. *Protestant, Catholic, Jew*. New York: Doubleday, 1955.

HOFFER, ERIC. *The True Believer*. New York: Harper and Bros., 1951.

HOFFMANN, STANLEY. *Le Mouvement Poujade*. Paris: Librairie Armand Colin, 1956.

HOFSTADTER, RICHARD. *The Age of Reform*. New York: Knopf, 1955.

HOOVER, CALVIN B. *Germany Enters the Third Reich*. New York: Macmillan, 1933.

HOWE, IRVING, and COSER, LEWIS. *The American Communist Party*. Boston: Beacon Press, 1957.

HOWE, IRVING, and WIDICK, B. J. *The UAW and Walter Reuther*. New York: Random House, 1949.

HYMAN, HERBERT, and SHEATSLEY, PAUL. "Trends in Public Opinion on Civil Liberties," *Journal of Social Issues*, IX (1953), 6-16.

HYMAN, HERBERT, and SHEATSLEY, PAUL. "The Authoritarian Personality—A Methodological Critique," in *Studies in the Scope and Method of "The Authoritarian Personality,"* ed. RICHARD CHRISTIE and MARIE JAHODA, pp. 50-122. Glencoe: The Free Press, 1954.

Italian Political Party Preferences. A report prepared for the Center for International Studies of M. I. T. Unpublished MS, 1953.

JANOWITZ, MORRIS. "Social Stratification and Mobility in West Germany," *The American Journal of Sociology*, LXIV (1958), 6-24.

JANOWITZ, MORRIS, and MARVICK, DWAINE. "Authoritarianism and Political Behavior," *Public Opinion Quarterly*, XVII (1953), 185-201.

JANOWITZ, MORRIS, and MARVICK, DWAINE. *Competitive Pressures and Democratic Consent*. Ann Arbor: University of Michigan Press, 1956.

DE JOUVENEL, BERTRAND. *Power*. London: Batchworth Press, 1952.

KAUFMAN, HAROLD. "Prestige Classes in a New York Rural Community," in *Class, Status and Power*, ed. REINHARD BENDIX and S. M. LIPSET, pp. 190-203. Glencoe: The Free Press, 1953.

KENNAN, GEORGE F. "Totalitarianism in the Modern World," in *Totalitarianism*, ed. CARL J. FRIEDRICH, pp. 17-36. Cambridge: Harvard University Press, 1954.

KERR, CLARK. "Industrial Relations and the Liberal Pluralist," in *Proceedings of the Seventh Annual Meeting of the Industrial Relations Research Association*, ed. L. REED TRUPP, pp. 2-16. Madison: Industrial Relations Research Association, 1955.

KERR, CLARK, and SIEGEL, A. "The Interindustry Propensity to Strike—An International Comparison," in *Industrial Conflict*, ed. ARTHUR KORNHAUSER, R. DUBIN, and A. ROSS, pp. 189-212. New York: McGraw Hill, 1954.

KEY, V. O. *Southern Politics*. New York: Knopf, 1949.

KEY, V. O. *Politics, Parties and Pressure Groups*. New York: Thomas Y. Crowell, 1952.

KIRCHHEIMER, OTTO. "West German Trade-Unions: Their Domestic and Foreign Policies," in *West German Leadership and Foreign Policy*, ed. HANS SPEIER and W. PHILLIPS DAVISON, pp. 282-304. Evanston: Row, Peterson, 1957.

KIRK, RUSSELL. *Prospects for Conservatives*. Chicago: Gateway Books, 1956.

KNIGHT, M. *The German Executive*. Stanford: Stanford University Press, 1952.

KOESTLER, ARTHUR. *Darkness at Noon*. New York: Macmillan Co., 1941.

KOMAROVSKY, MIRRA. *The Unemployed Man and His Family*. New York: Dryden, 1940.

KOMAROVSKY, MIRRA. "The Voluntary Association of Urban Dwellers," in *Sociological Analysis*, ed. LOGAN WILSON and W. KOLB, pp. 378-92. New York: Harcourt, Brace, 1949.

KORNHAUSER, ARTHUR; SHEPPARD, H.; and MAYER, A. *When Labor Votes: A Study of Auto Workers*. New York: University Books, 1956.

KOTSCHNIG, WALTER. *Unemployment in the Learned Professions*. London: Oxford University Press, 1937.

KRUGMAN, HERBERT E. "The Appeal of Communism to American Middle Class Intellectuals and Trade Unionists," *Public Opinion Quarterly*, XVI (1952), 331-55.

LANE, ROBERT E. "Political Personality and Electoral Choice," *American Political Science Review*, XLIX (1955), 173-79.

LASKI, HAROLD J. *Authority in the Modern State*. New Haven: Yale University Press, 1919.

LASSWELL, HAROLD D. "The Psychology of Hitlerism," *Political Quarterly*, IV (1933), 373-84.

LASSWELL, HAROLD D. "The Garrison State," *The American Journal of Sociology*, XLVI (1941), 455-68.

LASSWELL, HAROLD D. *The Analysis of Political Behavior*. London: Kegan Paul, 1947.

LASSWELL, HAROLD D., and BLUMENSTOCK, H. *World Revolutionary Propaganda*. New York: Knopf, 1939.

LASSWELL, HAROLD D., and KAPLAN, ABRAHAM. *Power and Society*. New Haven:: Yale University Press, 1950.

LASSWELL, HAROLD D.; LERNER, DANIEL; and ROTHWELL, E. E. *The Comparative Study of Elites*. Stanford: Stanford University Press, 1952.

LAZARSFELD, PAUL; BERELSON, B.; and GAUDET, H. *The People's Choice*. New York: Duell, Sloan, and Pearce, 1948.

LE BON, GUSTAVE. *The Crowd*. London: Ernest Bonn Ltd., 1947.

LEDERER, EMIL. *State of the Masses*. New York: W. W. Norton, 1940.

LENIN, V. I. *What Is To Be Done?* New York: International Publishers, 1929.

LERNER, DANIEL. *The Nazi Elite*. Stanford: Stanford University Press, 1951.

LERNER, DANIEL. "The 'Hard-Headed' Frenchman," *Encounter*, VIII (March, 1957), 27-32.

LEWINSON, RICHARD. *Das Geld in der Politik*. Berlin: Fischer Verlag, 1930.

LINDSAY, A. D. *The Modern Democratic State*. Vol. I. London: Oxford University Press, 1943.

LINZ, JUAN. "The Social Bases of West German Politics." Unpublished Ph.D. dissertation, Columbia University, 1958.

LIPPMANN, WALTER. *The Public Philosophy*. New York: Mentor Books, 1956.

LIPSET, S. M. "The Sources of the 'Radical Right,'" in *The New American Right*, ed. DANIEL BELL, pp. 166-233. New York: Criterion Books, 1955.

LIPSET, S. M. "The Working Class and Democratic Values." Unpublished MS, n. d.

LIPSET, S. M.; LAZARSFELD, P.; BARTON, A.; and LINZ, J. "The Psychology of Voting: An Analysis of Political Behavior," in *Handbook of Social Psychology*, Vol. II, *Special Fields and Applications*, ed. GARDNER LINDZEY, pp. 1124-75. Cambridge: Addison-Wesley, 1954.

LIPSET, S. M., and LINZ, JUAN. *The Social Bases of Political Diversity in Western Democracies*. Unpublished MS, 1956.

LIPSET, S. M.; TROW, M.; and COLEMAN, J. *Union Democracy*. Glencoe: The Free Press, 1956.

LOCHNER, LOUIS P. *Tycoon and Tyrant: German Industry from Hitler to Adenauer*. Chicago: Henry Regnery, 1954.

LOOMIS, CHARLES P., and BEAGLE, A. "The Spread of German Nazism in Rural Areas," *American Sociological Review*, XI (1946), 724-34.

LORWIN, VAL. *The French Labor Movement*. Cambridge: Harvard University Press, 1954.

LORWIN, VAL. "Working-Class Politics and Economic Development in Western Europe," *American Historical Review*, LXIII (1958), 338-57.

LOUCKS, EMERSON H. *The Ku Klux Klan in Pennsylvania*. Harrisburg: Telegraph Press, 1936.

LUETHY, HERBERT. "Poujade: Hitler or Pierrot?," *Commentary*, XXI (April, 1956), 301-10.

LUETHY, HERBERT. *France Against Herself*. New York: Meridian Books, 1957.

LYND, ROBERT M. and LYND, H. *Middletown*. New York: Harcourt, Brace, 1929.

MCCALLUM, RONALD B., and READMAN, ALISON. *The British General Election of 1945*. London: Oxford University Press, 1947.

MACKINNON, W. J. and CENTERS, R. "Authoritarianism and Urban Stratification," *The American Journal of Sociology*, LXI (1956), 610-20.

MCWILLIAMS, CAREY. *Factories in the Field*. Boston: Little, Brown, 1939.

DE MAN, HENRI. *Psychology of Socialism.* New York: Henry Holt and Co., 1927.

MANN, GOLO. "The German Intellectuals," *Encounter,* IV (June, 1955), 42-49.

MANNHEIM, KARL. *Ideology and Utopia.* London: Routledge and Kegan Paul, 1936.

MANNHEIM, KARL. *Man and Society in an Age of Reconstruction.* London: Kegan Paul, 1940.

MANNHEIM, KARL. *Essays on Sociology and Social Psychology.* New York: Oxford University Press, 1953.

MARX, KARL. *Capital.* New York: Random House, n. d.

MATHER, W. C. "Income and Social Participation," *American Sociological Review,* VI (1941), 380-3.

MATTHEWS, DONALD R. *The Social Background of Political Decision-Makers.* Garden City: Doubleday, 1954.

MERTON, ROBERT K. "Social Structure and Anomie," in *Social Theory and Social Structure,* by ROBERT K. MERTON, pp. 131-60. Glencoe: The Free Press, 1957.

MICHELS, ROBERT. *Political Parties.* Glencoe: The Free Press, 1949.

MICKLEN, JOHN M. *The Ku Klux Klan: A Study of the American Mind.* New York: Harcourt, Brace, 1924.

MILLS, C. WRIGHT. *The New Men of Power.* New York: Harcourt, Brace, 1948.

MILLS, C. WRIGHT. *White Collar.* New York: Oxford University Press, 1951.

MILLS, C. WRIGHT. *The Power Elite.* New York: Oxford University Press, 1956.

MONNEROT, JULES. *Sociology and Psychology of Communism.* Boston: Beacon Press, 1953.

NEUMANN, FRANZ. *European Trade Unionism and Politics.* New York: League for Industrial Democracy, 1936.

NEUMANN, FRANZ. *Behemoth: The Structure and Practice of National Socialism, 1933-1944.* New York: Oxford University Press, 1944.

NEUMANN, FRANZ. *The Democratic and the Authoritarian State.* Glencoe: The Free Press, 1957.

NEUMANN, SIGMUND. *Permanent Revolution.* New York: Harper and Bros., 1942.

NISBET, ROBERT A. *The Quest for Community.* New York: Oxford University Press, 1953.

NOMAD, MAX. *Rebels and Renegades.* New York: Macmillan Co., 1932.

ORTEGA Y GASSET, JOSE. *The Revolt of the Masses.* New York: W. W. Norton, 1932.

OVERACKER, LOUISE. *The Australian Party System.* New Haven: Yale University Press, 1952.

PARK, ROBERT E. *Human Communities.* Glencoe: The Free Press, 1952.

PARSONS, TALCOTT. "Some Sociological Aspects of the Fascist Movement," *Social Forces,* XXI (1942), 138-47.

PELLING, HENRY. *The British Communist Party.* London: A. & C. Black, 1958.

PETERSON, EDWARD. *Hjalmar Schacht: For and Against Hitler; A Politico-Economic Study of Germany, 1923-1949.* Boston: Christopher Publishing House, 1954.

POLLOCK, JAMES K., *et al. British Election Studies, 1950.* Ann Arbor: George Wahr, 1951.

PRATT, SAMUEL. "The Social Basis of Nazism and Communism in Urban Germany." Unpublished Master's thesis, Michigan State College, 1938.

Public Opinion Quarterly. "The Quarter's Polls," ed. MILDRED STRUNK. Vol. XIII (1949), 154-76.

RADKEY, OLIVER H. *The Election to the Russian Constituent Assembly of 1917.* Cambridge: Harvard University Press, 1950.

RAUSCHNING, HERMÁNN. *The Revolution of Nihilism.* New York: Alliance Book Corp., 1939.

REIWALD, PAUL. *De L'Esprit des Masses.* Neuchatel and Paris: Delachaux and Nicstlé, 1949.

RIESMAN, DAVID. In collaboration with NATHAN GLAZER and REUEL DENNEY. *The Lonely Crowd.* Abridged edition. Garden City: Doubleday, 1953.

ROSE, ARNOLD J. *Theory and Method in the Social Sciences.* Minneapolis: University of Minnesota Press, 1954.

ROSENBERG, BERNARD, and WHITE, DAVID (eds.). *Mass Culture.* Glencoe: The Free Press, 1957.

ROSSI, A. *The Rise of Italian Fascism, 1918-1922.* London: Methuen and Co., 1938.

SALVEMINI, GAETANO. *The Fascist Dictatorship in Italy.* New York: Henry Holt, 1927.

SAPOSS, DAVID J. "Current Trade-Union Movements of Western Europe," *Social Research,* XXI (1954), 297-313.

SCHORSKE, CARL E. *German Social Democracy 1905-17, The Development of the Great Schism.* Cambridge: Harvard University Press, 1955.

SCHUELLER, GEORGE K. *The Politburo.* Stanford: Stanford University Press, 1951.

SCHUMPETER, JOSEPH. *Capitalism, Socialism, and Democracy.* New York: Harper and Bros., 1947.

SCHWEITZER, ARTHUR. "The Nazification of the Lower Middle Class and Peasants," in *The Third Reich,* ed. MAURICE BAUMONT *et al.,* pp. 576-94. New York: Praeger, 1955.

SELZNICK, PHILIP. *The Organizational Weapon.* New York: McGraw-Hill, 1952.

SELZNICK, PHILIP. *Leadership in Administration.* Evanston: Row, Peterson, 1957.

SHILS, EDWARD A. "Authoritarianism: 'Right' and 'Left,' " in *Studies in the Scope and Method of "The Authoritarian Personality,"* ed. RICHARD CHRISTIE and MARIE JAHODA, pp. 24-49. Glencoe: The Free Press, 1954.

SHILS, EDWARD A. "Populism and the Rule of Law," *University of Chicago Law School Conference on Jurisprudence and Politics,* April, 1954, pp. 91-107.

SHILS, EDWARD A. *The Torment of Secrecy.* Glencoe: The Free Press, 1956.

SIMMEL, GEORG. "The Metropolis and Mental Life," in *The Sociology of Georg Simmel,* ed. KURT WOLFF, pp. 409-24. Glencoe: The Free Press, 1950.

SIMMEL, GEORG. *Conflict and the Web of Group-Affiliation.* Glencoe: The Free Press, 1955.

SOREL, GEORGES. *Reflections on Violence.* Glencoe: The Free Press, 1950.

SPARGO, JOHN. *The Psychology of Bolshevism.* New York: Harper and Bros., 1919.

SPEIER, HANS. *The Salaried Employee in German Society.* New York: WPA and Department of Social Science, Columbia University, 1939.

STOETZEL, J. "Voting Behavior in France," *British Journal of Sociology,* VI (1955), 104-22.

STOUFFER, SAMUEL A. *Communism, Conformity and Civil Liberties.* Garden City: Doubleday, 1955.

SUMNER, B. H. *A Short History of Russia.* New York: Harcourt, Brace, 1949.

TALMON, J. L. *The Rise of Totalitarian Democracy.* Boston: Beacon Press, 1952.

TAYLOR, A. J. P. "Manchester," *Encounter,* VIII (March, 1957), 3-13.

THYSSEN, F. *I Paid Hitler.* New York: Farrar and Rinehart, 1941.

DE TOCQUEVILLE, ALEXIS. *Democracy in America.* 2 vols. New York: Knopf, 1945.

DE TOCQUEVILLE, ALEXIS. *The Old Régime and the French Revolution.* Garden City: Doubleday, 1955.

TONNIES, FERDINAND. *Fundamental Concepts of Sociology (Gemeinschaft und Gesellschaft).* New York: American Book Co., 1940.

TOWSTER, JULIAN. *Political Power in the U.S.S.R., 1917-1947.* New York: Oxford University Press, 1948.

TREVELYAN, G. M. *History of England.* Vol. I, *From the Earliest Times to the Reformation.* Garden City: Doubleday, 1953.

TROTSKY, LEON. *The History of the Russian Revolution.* New York: Simon and Schuster, 1932.

TROW, MARTIN. "Small Businessmen, Political Tolerance, and Support for McCarthy," *The American Journal of Sociology,* LXIV (1958), 270-81.

TRUMAN, DAVID. *The Governmental Process.* New York: Knopf, 1951.

TURNER, RALPH, and KILLIAN, LEWIS M. *Collective Behavior*. Englewood Cliffs: Prentice-Hall, 1957.

UNITED NATIONS. STATISTICAL OFFICE. *Statistical Papers, Series E, No. 1: National and Per Capita Incomes of Seventy Countries in 1949 Expressed in United States Dollars*. New York: United Nations, 1950.

UNITED NATIONS. STATISTICAL OFFICE. *Statistical Yearbook, 1948*. Lake Success, N. Y.: United Nations, 1949.

UNITED NATIONS. STATISTICAL OFFICE. *Statistical Yearbook, 1955*. New York: United Nations, 1955.

U. S. DEPARTMENT OF STATE. OFFICE OF INTELLIGENCE RESEARCH. *The World Strength of the Communist Party*. January 1956.

USEEM, JOHN; TANGENT, P.; and USEEM, R. "Stratification in a Prairie Town," in *Sociological Analysis*, ed. LOGAN WILSON and W. KOLB, pp. 454-64. New York: Harcourt, Brace, 1949.

VIERECK, PETER. "The Revolt Against the Elite," in *The New American Right*, ed. DANIEL BELL, pp. 91-116. New York: Criterion Books, 1955.

VIERECK, PETER. *Conservatism from John Adams to Churchill*. New York: D. Van Nostrand, 1956.

WARNER, W. LLOYD, and LUNT, P. *The Social Life of a Modern Community*. New Haven: Yale University Press, 1941.

WEBER, MAX. *Essays in Sociology*. Edited by H. H. GERTH and C. W. MILLS. New York: Oxford University Press, 1946.

WEBER, MAX. *The Theory of Social and Economic Organization*. New York: Oxford University Press, 1947.

WHYTE, WILLIAM H. *The Organization Man*. New York: Doubleday, 1957.

WILLIAMS, PHILIP. *Politics in Post-War France*. London: Longmans, Green, 1954.

WIRTH, LOUIS. *Community Life and Social Policy*. Chicago: University of Chicago Press, 1956.

WOLFE, BERTRAM D. *Three Who Made a Revolution*. New York: Dial Press, 1948.

WOLFSON, MANFRED. "The SS Leadership." Unpublished MS, n. d.

WOODWARD, J. L. and ROPER, E. "Political Activity of American Citizens," *American Political Science Review*, XLIV (1950), 872-85.

WORLD HEALTH ORGANIZATION. *Epidemiological and Vital Statistics Report*. Vol. IX, no. 4 (1956).

WRIGHT, CHARLES R., and HYMAN, HERBERT. "Voluntary Association Memberships of American Adults: Evidence from National Sample Surveys," *American Sociological Review*, XXIII (1958), 284-94.

WRIGHT, GORDAN. "Agrarian Syndicalism in Postwar France," *American Political Science Review*, XLVII (1953), 402-16.

ZAWADSKI, BOHAN, and LAZARSFELD, PAUL. "The Psychological Consequences of Unemployment," *Journal of Social Psychology*, VI (1935), 224-51.

Index

Cambell, A., 72
Cantril, H., 69, 72, 180, 209
Capitalism, and fascism, 197, 198, 204
Centers, R., 69
Centralization, 75, 86, 89, 93–101, 234, 235
Chamberlin, W. H., 169
Civil liberties, support for, see Libertarianism
Cohn, N., 57, 58, 145, 146, 157, 214
Cole, G. D. H., 96
Coleman, J. S., 36, 59, 66, 67, 97
Communal society: conditions of, 39, 40, 63; culture of, 104, 105; intermediate structure of, 83, 84, 100; political rule in, 131; psychological properties of, 110, 111
Communist movements: activity of members of, 167; class appeal of, 48, 179, 180, 196; intellectuals' support for, 185, 186, 192, 193; mass appeal of, 14, 15, 48–50, 177–82, 196; middle-class support for, 194–96; peasant support for, 207, 209; totalitarian character of, 15, 46–49, 63, 123; working-class support for, 150–57, 180, 195, 213–21 (see also C.G.T., CIO, Trade unions, Unemployment); see also Communist vote
Communist vote: and degree of industrialization, 150; and degree of urbanization, 143, 144; and Fascist vote, 124; following World War II, 171, 172; and per capita income, 160–62; and rates of alcoholism, homicide, and suicide, 91, 92; and socialist vote, 124, 160; and unemployment, 160–63, 166, 167; see also Communist movement
Community: discontinuities in, 125, 142–58; loss of, 30–34, 120; participation in, see Participation; see also Non-elites
C.G.T., Communist penetration of, 147, 213
CIO, Communist penetration of, 146, 147, 214
Conservative parties: class composition of, 194, 195; distinguished from Fascist movements, 122
Constitutionalism, 130–32, 134, 135
Coser, L., 54, 180
Crossman, R., 185

Dahl, R., 130
Davison, W. P., 92, 157, 178, 179, 217, 218, 220
DeGré, G., 43

Democracy: liberal, 131, 132; populist, 130–32; social conditions of liberal, 138–41, 229–38 (see also Pluralism); social effects of, 126, 130, 172, 238; see also Constitutionalism, Equalitarianism, Liberty
Denmark, industrialization and the labor movement in, 153, 154
Depression, and mass movements, 160–67, 174 (see also Unemployment)
Doerne, M., 188
Domenach, J., 151, 155
Durkheim, E., 63, 76, 78, 79, 88
Dynes, R. R., 73

Ebenstein, W., 137, 138, 169, 170
Education: of elites compared to non-elites, 56, 57; and libertarianism, see Libertarianism; and participation, see Participation
Ehrmann, H., 209, 219
Einaudi, M., 151, 155
Eisenberg, P., 164
Eliot, T. S., 26
Elites: access to, 20, 22, 23, 26–30, 34–43, 51–60, 77, 78, 81, 82, 99, 100, 131, 234–36; activism of, 34–36; alienation of, see Alienation; atomization of, see Atomization; competition among, 55; definition of, 51; and democracy, 52, 236; education of, see Education; impact of depression on, 167; impact of war on, 168–72; social composition of political, 53, 54, 56, 183, 184; types of, 54; see also Authority, Intellectuals and professionals, Upper classes
England; see Great Britain
Equalitarianism: aristocratic view of, 22, 23, 26–29, 31, 119, 120; democratic view of, 23, 30–32, 120; Marxist view of, 139, 140
Ethnic groups, and Communism, 180, 218

Fainsod, M., 169, 191
Family, isolation of, 90–93, 164 (see also Primary groups)
Farmers: and Communist movements, 207, 209; and Fascist movements, 162, 207–10; isolation of, 208–10; organization of, 208, 209; xenophobia of, 209, 210; see also Farm laborers
Farm laborers: and Communist movements, 219; and Fascist movements, 219; isolation of, 218, 219